CAMPAIGN 375

EAST CHINA SEA 1945

Climax of the Kamikaze

BRIAN LANE HERDER

ILLUSTRATED BY ADAM TOOBY
Series editor Nikolai Bogdanovic

OSPREY PUBLISHING
Bloomsbury Publishing Plc
Kemp House, Chawley Park, Cumnor Hill, Oxford OX2 9PH, UK
29 Earlsfort Terrace, Dublin 2, Ireland
1385 Broadway, 5th Floor, New York, NY 10018, USA
E-mail: info@ospreypublishing.com
www.ospreypublishing.com

OSPREY is a trademark of Osprey Publishing Ltd

First published in Great Britain in 2022

© Osprey Publishing Ltd, 2022

A catalogue record for this book is available from the British Library.

ISBN: PB 9781472848468; eBook 9781472848475; ePDF 9781472848352; XML 9781472848345

22 23 24 25 26 10 9 8 7 6 5 4 3 2 1

Maps by Bounford.com
3D BEVs by Paul Kime
Index by Angela Hall
Typeset by PDQ Digital Media Solutions, Bungay, UK
Printed and bound in India by Replika Press Private Ltd.

Artist's note

Readers can find out more about the work of battlescene illustrator Adam Tooby at the following website: http://www.adamtooby.com

Title page: HMS *Formidable* shortly after being crashed by a Zero at 1131hrs, May 4, 1945. (© Imperial War Museum, A 29717)
Front cover artwork: Sub-Lieutenant Richard Reynolds, flying a Seafire III, defends HMS *Indefatigable* off the Sakishima Gunto, April 1, 1945. (Adam Tooby)

Osprey Publishing supports the Woodland Trust, the UK's leading woodland conservation charity.

To find out more about our authors and books visit **www.ospreypublishing.com**. Here you will find extracts, author interviews, details of forthcoming events and the option to sign up for our newsletter.

Author's dedication

This book is dedicated to my brilliant, handsome, and fun-loving father Lloyd Dale Herder (October 29, 1948–September 10, 2021). You taught me to love knowledge, education, family, adventure, and the American West. I love you and miss you terribly. You died 20 years too early.

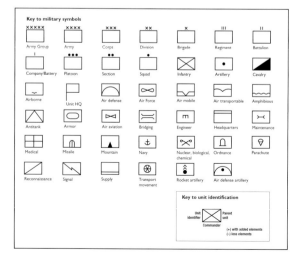

CONTENTS

The East China Sea in 1945

INTRODUCTION

THE STRATEGIC SETTING

By 1945 the United States' methodical Central Pacific counteroffensive was closing in on Japan itself. Forcing the Empire's unconditional surrender would require either a crushing air–sea blockade and bombardment of the Home Islands or else a direct ground invasion into Tokyo. Whichever strategic option US planners ultimately chose, both would require major bases ringing southern Japan that would ensure US domination of the East China Sea.

In pursuit of these endgame bases, in early 1945 the United States staged twin amphibious campaigns for the islands of Iwo Jima and Okinawa. As the ensuing ground combat has been well covered in Osprey's *Iwo Jima 1945* and *Okinawa 1945*, this book addresses the epic air–sea actions that raged both in support and defiance of the American landings. The associated numbers are truly massive. At over 1,600 ships, the Okinawa invasion armada was arguably the largest fleet of all time. Meanwhile, although the Japanese had first unleashed kamikaze attacks in the Philippines in October 1944, in terms of sheer scale and intensity the suicide bombardment would climax the following year in the East China Sea. From February through June 1945, Japan would expend over 2,000 kamikazes off Iwo Jima, Okinawa, and the Home Islands in the greatest sustained air–sea onslaught in history.

Japanese suicide attacks involved not just the standard kamikaze of Anglo-American legend, but increasingly sophisticated, purpose-built weapons such as the *Ohka* (suicide rocket), *Shinyo* (suicide boat), and *Kaiten* (suicide torpedo). The greatest *tokko* ("special" or suicide) attack of all was Operation *Ten-Ichi-Go*, the forlorn April 6–7, 1945 sortie of the superbattleship *Yamato* and her escorts against the Okinawa invasion force.

The late-war mass kamikaze attacks remain shocking for their ferocity, violence, and downright eeriness. A US officer later explained: "I doubt there is

Early in the morning on February 23, 1945 a detachment from the 28th Marines fought their way up Iwo Jima's Suribachi volcano and planted their small regimental US flag atop the summit, inspiring a raucous celebration among the US fleet anchored offshore. Hours later, the marines were ordered to replace it with a larger flag from *LST-779*. Correspondent Joe Rosenthal's photograph of the second flag raising, seen here, became one of the iconic images of World War II. (Photo by Joe Rosenthal/Photo 12/Universal Images Group via Getty Images)

anyone who can depict ... our mixed emotions as we watched a man about to die in order that he might destroy himself in the process. There was a hypnotic fascination to a sight so alien in our Western philosophy."

ORIGINS OF THE CAMPAIGN

On June 15, 1944, the United States' Operation *Forager* invaded the Japanese-occupied Marianas Islands, securing them by August 10. US planners then targeted the Philippines' Leyte, to be invaded by General Douglas MacArthur's South-West Pacific forces on October 20, 1944. Concerning post-Leyte operations, USN chief Admiral Ernest King pushed strongly for Operation *Causeway*, which would land Lieutenant-General Simon Bolivar Buckner Jr.'s newly established US Tenth Army in Formosa, the Pescadores Islands, and the China coast near Amoy on March 1, 1945.

In contrast, King's Fifth Fleet commander, Vice Admiral Raymond Spruance, supported capturing Iwo Jima and Okinawa. As an airfield halfway between Tokyo and the Marianas, Iwo Jima could support Spruance's carriers against Japan. By occupying Okinawa, US forces could control the East China Sea while developing a major forward staging base against the Home Islands. Spruance quickly won over the US Pacific Fleet commander, Admiral Chester Nimitz. Desiring both islands for airbases, the USAAF also approved—as early as 1944 the USAAF planned to stage five P-51 Fighter Groups from Iwo Jima to escort B-29 raids against Japan. Most importantly, by September 1944 the seemingly beaten German Wehrmacht had unexpectedly rallied, dashing Allied expectations of an early victory in Europe. Unlike Formosa, Iwo Jima and Okinawa could be assaulted with forces already in the Pacific. Spruance would take Iwo Jima first, as it would be much easier to isolate from Japanese airpower than Okinawa.

On October 3, 1944, the US Joint Chiefs of Staff canceled *Causeway* and authorized the sequential invasions of Luzon, Iwo Jima, and Okinawa after Leyte. By January 1945, Leyte's airfield construction delays had pushed the invasion of Iwo Jima, codenamed Operation *Detachment*, to February 19, 1945, while delaying the invasion of Okinawa, codenamed Operation *Iceberg*, to April 1, 1945.

Iwo Jima, in easy range of the Marianas, had first been attacked on June 15 and June 24, 1944, by Rear Admiral J.J. Jocko Clark's fast carrier Task Group TG-58.1. Meanwhile, USAAF raids and USN shellings of Iwo Jima began in August 1944. They would grow steadily in strength and frequency into February 1945.

US naval and amphibious forces mass at Ulithi atoll, late 1944. In 1945 much of the Okinawa invasion fleet sailed from Ulithi, although the Northern Tractor Flotilla came from Guadalcanal and the Southern Tractor Flotilla departed from Leyte. Rear Admiral Jerauld Wright's Demonstration Group sortied from Saipan with the 2nd Marine Division and just barely made H-Hour. (NARA via Mighty90)

CHRONOLOGY

1945

February 16	Spruance's US Fifth Fleet begins *Detachment* pre-landing bombardment.
February 16–17, 25	Mitscher's TF-58 strikes Tokyo in support of *Detachment*.
February 19	*Detachment* D-Day; Schmidt's US V Amphibious Corps lands on Iwo Jima.
March 1	TF-58 strikes Okinawa.
March 18–19	TF-58 strikes Inland Sea in support of *Iceberg*.
March 25	US Fifth Fleet begins *Iceberg* pre-landing bombardment.
March 26	Iwo Jima secured; British TF-57 commences *Iceberg* combat operations.
March 26–29	US 77th Division assaults and captures Kerama Retto; *Ten-Go* activated.
March 31	US 420th Field Artillery lands on Keise Shima.
April 1	*Iceberg* L-Day; Buckner's US Tenth Army lands on Okinawa.
April 2	US XXIV Corps reaches east coast, severs Okinawa.
April 6–7	*Kikisui* No. 1 and *Ten-Ichi-Go*.
April 7	*Yamato*, *Yahagi*, and four IJN destroyers sunk by TF-58 aircraft.
April 12–13	*Kikisui* No. 2.
April 15–16	*Kikisui* No. 3, TF-58 strikes Kyushu.
April 16–21	US 77th Infantry Division assaults and captures Ie Shima.
April 27–28	*Kikisui* No. 4.
May 3–4	*Kikisui* No. 5.
May 10–11	*Kikisui* No. 6.
May 13–14	TF-58 strikes Kyushu and Shikoku.
May 23–25	*Kikisui* No. 7.
May 25	TF-57 concludes *Iceberg* operations.
May 27	Halsey relieves Spruance; Fifth Fleet becomes Third Fleet.
May 27–29	*Kikisui* No. 8.
June 2–3	TF-38 strikes Kyushu.
June 3–7	*Kikisui* No. 9.
June 4–5	TF-38 blunders into Typhoon Viper.
June 8	TF-38 strikes Kyushu.
June 10	TF-38 concludes *Iceberg* operations.
June 21–22	*Kikisui* No. 10.
July 2	Okinawa declared secure.

OPPOSING COMMANDERS

JAPANESE

As 1945 dawned, the despondent Japanese high command (Imperial General Headquarters—IGHQ) steeled itself to face the inevitable American assault on Japan's inner defense sphere. Too late, IGHQ took the radical measure of formalizing Japanese inter-service coordination. The subsequent joint IJN/IJA *Ten-Go* operations plan of February 6, 1945 stated: "The basic command relationship will be one of inter-service cooperation. Coordination will be affected through Combined Fleet for the Navy Air Forces, and through the General Defense Command and Tenth Area Army for the Army Air Forces."

Vice Admiral Matome Ugaki assumed command of Kyushu's IJN Fifth Air Fleet (*Dai-Go Koku Kantai*) on February 10, 1945. IGHQ additionally assigned Ugaki control over all Kyushu-based East China Sea air operations. A moody and fatalistic widower, Ugaki had grown increasingly bipolar as the war progressed. Hours after Japan surrendered, on August 15, 1945, a guilt-laden Ugaki would embark on the war's last kamikaze mission, only to be duly shot down off Okinawa.

Yamato officers pose for a group photo before *Ten-Ichi-Go*. Ito is third from left in the front row. Ito's chief-of-staff, Rear Admiral Nobuei Morishita, is third from the right in the front row, and was *Ten-Ichi-Go*'s highest-ranking survivor. Ito was on the verge of proposing Second Fleet be deactivated and its personnel moved ashore for homeland defense when the *Yamato* mission was ordered. (Public Domain)

Ugaki's close friend **Vice Admiral Kinpei Teraoka** commanded Honshu's Third Air Fleet (*Dai-San Koku Kantai*), which would intensively train in *tokko* tactics before redeploying to Kyushu for *Ten-Go*. In late April they would be joined by IJN Tenth Air Fleet (*Dai-Ju Koku Kantai*), established March 1, 1945 under **Vice Admiral Minoru Maeda**. The final *Ten-Go* air force transferred to Kyushu was the IJAAF's Sixth Air Army (*Koku Gun*), commanded by **Lieutenant-General Michio Sugahara** and temporarily subordinated under Ugaki's operational command on March 21, 1945.

Ten-Go's Formosa air forces remained independent of Ugaki's control. Commanding Formosa's IJN First Air Fleet (*Daiichi Koku Kantai*) was **Vice Admiral Takijiro Onishi**, who had originally spearheaded Japan's turn to kamikaze tactics in 1944. After leaving a suicide note apologizing to the 4,000 kamikaze pilots whom he had sent to die, Onishi would commit *seppeku* (ritual disembowelment) on August 16, 1945. As penance to his former men, Onishi refused the customary *coup de grâce* from a second, only finally dying 15 agonizing hours later. Onishi's IJAAF counterpart was **Lieutenant-General Kenji Yamamoto**, who commanded Formosa's IJA 8th Air Division (*Hiko Shidan*).

Vice Admiral Seiichi Ito commanded the Kure-based IJN Second Fleet, the surface force defending the Home Islands. Ito was a long-time staff officer recently promoted to Second Fleet command. Ironically, Ito had opposed war with America and was regarded as a deep and sensitive thinker whose fighting spirit was questionable. Ito would fly his flag for the suicidal *Ten-Ichi-Go* from superbattleship *Yamato*, commanded by **Captain Kosaku Ariga**.

Rear Admiral Keizo Komura, riding light cruiser *Yahagi*, commanded *Ten-Ichi-Go*'s Second Destroyer Squadron. *Yahagi*'s skipper, **Captain Tameichi Hara**, had written the IJN's official torpedo attack doctrine in the 1930s. After seeing consistent Pacific War action, Hara ultimately became the only IJN destroyer captain to survive the entire war. Hara's 1967 memoirs, *Japanese Destroyer Captain*, provide much of the surviving strategic and planning history of *Ten-Ichi-Go*.

Vice Admiral Marc Mitscher (right) and his chief-of-staff, Commodore Arleigh Burke (left), plan Task Force 58's February 1945 Tokyo raids. These were intended to preempt Japanese aerial counterattacks against the Iwo Jima landings. (NHHC 80-G-303981)

ALLIED

The quiet, austere, and conservative **Admiral Raymond A. Spruance** commanded the powerful US Fifth Fleet; fellow US admirals nicknamed him "The Electric Brain" for his famously calculating mind. Always calm and equable, Spruance described kamikaze tactics as "very sound and economical war and a form especially suited to the Japanese temperament."

Veteran aviator **Vice Admiral Marc Mitscher** commanded Spruance's Fast Carrier Task Force, Task Force 58. Mitscher's TF-58 was divided into

Vice Admiral Richmond Kelly Turner, Task Force 51 commander. The colorful Turner was a former aviator and known for his high intelligence and exceedingly foul mouth. In August 1942 Turner had commanded the USN's very first amphibious invasion at Guadalcanal. Turner is seen here off Kwajalein in February 1944, still a rear admiral. (NHHC 80-G-216636)

four carrier Task Groups (TG-58.1, TG-58.2, TG-58.3, and TG-58.4), each commanded by an aviator rear admiral. The aggressive, competent Mitscher resembled Spruance in his calm, soft-spoken professionalism, and was accordingly well loved by his men. TF-58's Royal Navy counterpart was British Pacific Fleet fast carrier group Task Force 57, commanded by **Vice Admiral Sir Bernard Rawlings**. TF-57 was the product of intense and complex Anglo-American political wranglings. It would perform its *Iceberg* support mission semi-autonomously under Spruance's direction.

From amphibious command ship *Eldorado* (AGC-11), **Vice Admiral Richmond K. Turner** commanded Spruance's Joint Expeditionary Force, Task Force 51. Spruance tolerated Turner's alcoholism and violent temper because of Turner's demonstrated mastery of amphibious operations. Most of Fifth Fleet was subordinated within Turner's TF-51, including the Amphibious Support Force (TF-52) and the Attack Force(s) (TF-53 and TF-55).

Riding amphibious command ship *Estes* (AGC-12) was **Rear Admiral W.H.P. Blandy**, commander Amphibious Support Force (TF-52) and Turner's second-in-command at Okinawa. TF-52's mission was "to effect the maximum possible destruction of enemy forces and defenses by surface ship and aircraft bombardment, by minesweeping, and by underwater demolition" prior to the initial landings.

TF-52's varied requirements demanded diverse subordinate groups. Among these were the escort carriers and aircraft of **Rear Admiral Calvin T. Durgin**'s Support Carrier Group (designated TG-52.2 at Iwo Jima and TG-52.1 at Okinawa), the heavy gunships of the Gunfire and Covering Force (TF 54, commanded by **Rear Admiral Bertram Rodgers** at Iwo Jima and **Rear Admiral Morton Deyo** at Okinawa), and numerous other supporting groups and flotillas organized by type and mission, such as mine warfare or underwater demolition.

For Iwo Jima's *Detachment*, Turner's transports and landing ships fell under the Attack Force (TF-53), commanded by Turner's deputy **Rear Admiral Harry Hill**. TF-53 transported *Detachment*'s US V Amphibious Corps, commanded by **Major-General Harry Schmidt (USMC)**.

For Okinawa's much larger *Iceberg*, Turner expanded and divided the Attack Force into two separate forces, the Northern Attack Force (TF-53) under **Rear Admiral L.F. Reifsnider**, and the Southern Attack Force (TF-55) under **Rear Admiral J.L. Hall**. Together TF-53 and TF-55 embarked US Tenth Army, commanded by **Lieutenant-General Simon Buckner (US Army)**.

Spruance expected US aircraft to operate from Iwo Jima and Okinawa as soon as possible. Slated for Iwo Jima was the USAAF's VII Fighter Command, led by 37-year-old **Brigadier-General Ernest M. Moore (USAAF)**. Basing at Okinawa would be the specially established Tenth Army Tactical Air Force (TAF), commanded by **Major-General Francis C. Mulcahy (USMC)**.

OPPOSING FORCES

JAPANESE

Japanese air forces

Ten-Go assembled over 3,000 Japanese planes to attack US Fifth Fleet, plus another 300 Yokosuka MXY-7 *Ohka* suicide rockets. Kamikazes' enduring notoriety has greatly obscured the extensive and crucial role Japanese conventional air still played through 1945. Indeed, the poorly trained kamikazes had to be guided and escorted to the target by more experienced (and valuable) fighter pilots. Meanwhile, relatively modern, high-performance bombers such as the B6N Jill, P1Y Frances, Ki-67 Peggy, and D4Y Judy often attacked conventionally, including in nighttime raids, which a USN officer described as "witches on broomsticks."

A detailed description and analysis of Japanese *tokko* or kamikaze operations, tactics, and psychology is beyond the scope of this study. However, kamikazes offered certain advantages over conventional attacks. Kamikaze pilots were quicker, easier, and less expensive to train—as few as 30–50 flight hours for IJNAF kamikazes and just ten hours for IJAAF. Despite being terminally guided by human brains, kamikaze pilots were intelligent, resourceful, and evasive.

According to a March 1945 TF-58 report, "[Kamikaze] attacks were generally by single or few aircraft making their approaches with radical

This remarkable January 1945 photograph captures a suicidal Zero, still on course for its American target, despite being hit several times. The Zero ultimately crashed cruiser *Columbia*, killing 13 and wounding 44. The frustration of repeatedly hitting a diving kamikaze, only to have it slam into one's ship anyway, was a major aspect of kamikazes' inherently terrifying nature. (NHHC NH 79448)

Japan's wartime terminology exploited the distinctively poetic and euphemistic nature of the Japanese language. The informal term *kamikaze* actually means "divine wind." Specifically, *kamikaze* refers to the typhoons that miraculously wrecked Kublai Khan's Mongol–Koryo invasion fleets in 1274. Like "blitzkrieg", the unofficial term "kamikaze" was mostly used by Allied journalists. The IJN and IJA officially called suicide attack units *tokubetsu kogekitai*, meaning "special attack unit." This was usually shortened to *tokkutai*, with *tokko* both noun and adjective meaning "special" (i.e. suicide). *Kikisui* was the codename for the ten mass kamikaze attacks off Okinawa against the Allied fleet. *Kikisui* means "floating chrysanthemum," which was the war emblem of legendary 14th-century samurai Masashige Kusinoke, a national exemplar of sacrificial devotion to the Emperor.

changes in course and altitude, dispersing when intercepted and using cloud cover to every advantage. They tailed our friendlies home, used decoy planes, and came in at any altitude or on the water." After entering its terminal dive, defeating an attacking kamikaze usually required obliterating it, a tall order for either aircraft or guns. Although even bomb-laden kamikazes were too flimsy to sink a heavily armored warship, kamikazes' exploding shrapnel and flaming gasoline caused staggering physical and personnel damage topside and tended to produce horrific burn casualties.

Japanese naval forces

The Kure-based IJN Second Fleet comprised a nominal three battleships, two battleship-carriers, two heavy cruisers, two light cruisers, and 25 destroyers, while IJN Third Fleet comprised two large and three small carriers. Realistically, scarce petroleum, rampant disrepair, and a lack of trained carrier air groups meant only superbattleship *Yamato* and a destroyer squadron were still capable of operations.

Commissioned in 1941, the 71,659-ton *Yamato*, an ancient, poetic name for Japan, was the largest and most heavily armed and armored battleship in the world, mounting a main battery of nine 460mm (18.1in.) guns. At 27kts she could easily outrun Turner's old pre-war battleships, although not Mitscher's fast battleships. Accompanying *Yamato* were eight destroyers and the 6,652-ton Agano-class light cruiser *Yahagi*.

A captured Yokosuka MXY7 *Ohka* suicide rocket, photographed by the Americans on Okinawa on June 26, 1945. The *Ohka* (cherry blossom) was universally called the *Baka* (idiot) by the Americans. The best defense against the *Ohka* was to shoot down its lumbering Betty mothership before it could launch. (NHHC 80-G-K-5888)

By spring 1945, IJN Sixth Fleet retained approximately 15 operational fleet submarines. Some specially modified submarine motherships carried up to six 30kt piloted *Kaiten* suicide torpedoes, adapted from the Type 93 "Long Lance" and boasting a 3,420lb warhead.

ALLIED

By mid-March 1945, Spruance's Fifth Fleet comprised, in major front-line combatants alone, 40 aircraft carriers, 20 battleships, 31 cruisers, 181 destroyers, 61 destroyer-escorts, and 2,021 carrier aircraft.

Fifth Fleet's high-speed battle fleet and offensive spearhead was Mitscher's Fast Carrier Task Force (TF-58), which forward-deployed from the Carolines' Ulithi atoll. By February 1945, TF-58 comprised 17 fast carriers, eight fast battleships, 15 cruisers, 81 destroyers, and 1,170 modern carrier aircraft, including 853 F6F-5 Hellcat and F4U-1D/FG-1D Corsair fighters in 24 USN and four USMC squadrons. The remainder was made up of SB2C Helldiver dive-bombers and TBM Avenger torpedo bombers.

The Royal Navy's newly established fast carrier force, Rawlings' TF-57, forward-deployed from Leyte-Samar and comprised four fast carriers, fast battleships *Howe* and *King George V*, five cruisers, 11 destroyers, and 244 British- and American-built carrier aircraft.

Fifth Fleet's remaining combat formations comprised amphibious attack and support forces subordinated within Turner's TF-51. This staggering armada, over a thousand vessels, encompassed escort carriers, slow battleships, cruisers, destroyers, destroyer-escorts, transports, freighters, landing ships, hospital ships, minesweepers, minelayers, patrol boats, and a vast array of small support craft.

Providing American underway replenishment was Rear Admiral Donald Beary's Logistic Support Group Fifth Fleet (TG-50.8), comprising

Light cruiser *Flint* and several Essex-class fast carriers at Ulithi, March 1945. After striking Tokyo and supporting the Iwo Jima landings, Mitscher's Fast Carrier Task Force was resting and replenishing in preparation for the Okinawa invasion. The mobility and striking power of the fast carriers proved indispensable during *Iceberg*. (Navsource)

A 40mm Bofors antiaircraft crew drills aboard carrier *Hornet*, February 1945. A USN study called the Bofors the most effective naval antiaircraft gun of the war, but it would be sorely tested by the kamikaze threat. (NARA via Mighty90)

one cruiser flagship, 16 oilers, four ammunition ships, four fleet tugs, two airplane transports, two escort carriers, 12 destroyers, and seven destroyer-escorts. Replenishing the British TF-57 was the Royal Navy's Logistic Support Group (TG-112.2) of five escort carriers, four destroyers, four sloops, three frigates, five oilers, and four chartered merchantmen.

USN antiair defenses

American codebreaking, combined with shrewd Fifth Fleet signals work, helped anticipate mass kamikaze attacks. Air search radar was critical to detecting incoming Japanese airstrikes as early as possible. Carrier- and battleship-mounted SK-2 air search radars could detect incoming bogeys from about 80nm, allowing 16 minutes warning. Forward-deployed radar pickets, usually destroyers, extended overall fleet radar coverage outward from the fleet's center, but were highly exposed to attack. Fifth Fleet's first line of defense was its airborne fighter CAP (Combat Air Patrol), directed from shipboard Combat Information Centers by highly trained Fighter Directors. Backing CAPs were radar-directed American antiaircraft batteries, which by 1945 had become truly formidable in both density and accuracy.

In addition to the Task Groups' pickets, Turner ringed Okinawa with 15 permanent radar picket stations, each patrolled by an assigned destroyer that monitored nine radio channels and reported all contacts. Picket destroyers' SC air search radars could detect raids 50–75nm distant. Each picket embarked its own Fighter Director. Radar pickets were often escorted by a second destroyer and/or LCS and LCI craft armed with antiaircraft guns. Dedicated RAPCAP (Radar Picket Combat Air Patrol) fighters orbited in shifts over each picket station.

Island-based airpower

The Marianas-based USAAF VII Fighter Command would redeploy to Iwo Jima airfields as soon as possible. Iwo Jima's US air complement would eventually include 222 P-51D Mustangs of the 15th and 21st Fighter Groups, 24 P-61 Black Widows of the 548th and 549th Night Fighter Squadrons, and 18 TBM Avengers of the Marines' VMTB-242.

Slated for Okinawa, Tenth Army Tactical Air Force (TAF) comprised four USMC groups totaling 12 Corsair squadrons and three F6F-5N Hellcat night fighter squadrons, plus the USAAF's 301st Fighter Wing of the 318th, 413th, and 507th Fighter Groups. By June 30, TAF strength would exceed 750 aircraft.

The USN's Fleet Airwing One (FAW-1), headquartered aboard seaplane tender *Hamlin* (AV-15), would relocate to Iwo Jima between February 19 and March 10, 1945. FAW-1 would then redeploy to Okinawa's Kerama Retto on March 26, 1945.

OPERATION *ICEBERG* ORDERS OF BATTLE, APRIL 1, 1945

(Air/sea and antiair/sea forces only.)

JAPANESE

OKINAWA-BASED *TEN-GO* FORCES

IJA 32nd Army—Lieutenant-General Mitsuru Ushijima
21st Antiaircraft Artillery Group
    27th Independent Antiaircraft Artillery Battalion (75mm)
    70th, 80th, and 81st Field Antiaircraft Artillery Battalions
    (75mm)
    103rd, 104th, and 105th Independent Machine Cannon
    Battalions (20mm)
1st, 2nd, 3rd, and 4th Suicide Boat Regiments (Kerama Retto)
26th, 27th, 28th, and 29th Suicide Boat Regiments (Okinawa)
Okinawa Naval Base Force—Rear Admiral Minoru Ota
22nd and 42nd *Shinyo* Squadrons
1st, 2nd, and 3rd Surface Raiding Squadrons

HOME ISLANDS-BASED *TEN-GO* FORCES

IJN Third Air Fleet (*Dai-San Koku Kantai*)—Vice Admiral Kinpei Teraoka
25th Sentai
27th Sentai
131st Kokutai
210th Kokutai
252nd Kokutai
343rd Kokutai
601st Kokutai
706th Kokutai
722nd Kokutai
752nd Kokutai
1023rd Kokutai
IJN Fifth Air Fleet (*Dai-Go Koku Kantai*)—Vice Admiral Matome Ugaki
203rd Kokutai
701st Kokutai
721st Kokutai
762nd Kokutai
801st Kokutai
1022nd Kokutai
Kyushu Kokutai
Nansei-Shoto Kokutai
IJN Tenth Air Fleet (*Dai-Ju Koku Kantai*)—Vice Admiral Minoru Maeda
11th Rengo Kokutai
12th Rengo Kokutai
13th Rengo Kokutai
IJAAF Sixth Air Army (*Koku Gun*)—Lieutenant-General Michio Sugahara
12th Air Division (*Hiko Shidan*)
30th Fighter Group (*Hiko Sentai*)
IJN Special Surface Attack Force—Vice Admiral Seiichi Ito (*Yamato*)
Battleship *Yamato*
Second Destroyer Squadron—Rear Admiral Keizo Komura (*Yahagi*)
    Light cruiser *Yahagi*
    Destroyers *Fuyutsuki, Yukikaze, Hatsushimo, Asashimo, Kasumi,*
      Isokaze, Hamakaze

FORMOSA-BASED *TEN-GO* FORCES

IJAAF 8th Air Division (*Hiko Shidan*)—Lieutenant-General Kenji Yamamoto
IJN First Air Fleet (*Daiichi Koku Kantai*)—Vice Admiral Takijiro Onishi
26th Sentai (Air Flotilla)
Taiwan Kokutai
132nd Kokutai
133rd Kokutai
165th Kokutai
634th Kokutai
765th Kokutai
1021st Kokutai

ALLIES

US FIFTH FLEET—ADMIRAL RAYMOND SPRUANCE (*INDIANAPOLIS*)

Task Force 58 Fast Carrier Force—Vice Admiral Marc Mitscher (*Bunker Hill*)
Task Group 58.1—Rear Admiral J.J. "Jocko" Clark (*Hornet*)
Carrier *Hornet*
    VF-17: 71 F6F-5 Hellcat
    VB-17: 9 SB2C-3 Helldiver, 2 SB2C-4 Helldiver, 4 SBW Helldiver
    VT-17: 15 TBM-3 Avenger
Carrier *Bennington*
    VF-82: 37 F6F-5 Hellcat
    VB-82: 15 SB2C-4E Helldiver
    VT-82: 15 TBM-3 Avenger
    VMF-112: 18 F4U-1D Corsair
    VMF-123: 17 F4U-1D Corsair
Light carrier *Belleau Wood*
    VF-30: 24 F6F-5 Hellcat, one F6F-5P Hellcat
    VT-30: 8 TBM-3 Avenger, one TBM-3P Avenger
Light carrier *San Jacinto*
    VF-45: 25 F6F-5 Hellcat
    VT-45: 9 TBM-3 Avenger
Battleship Division 8—Rear Admiral John Shafroth
    Battleships *Massachusetts, Indiana*
Cruiser Division 10 (Wiltse)
    Heavy cruisers *Baltimore, Pittsburgh*
Cruiser Division 14 (Whiting)
    Light cruisers *Vincennes, Miami, Vicksburg, San Juan*
Destroyer Squadron 61
    Destroyer Division 121
        Destroyers *De Haven, Mansfield, Swenson, Collett, Maddox*
    Destroyer Division 122
        Destroyers *Blue, Brush, Taussig, Samuel N. Moore*
    Destroyer Division 106
        Destroyers *Wedderburn, Twining, Stockham*
Destroyer Squadron 25
    Destroyer Division 49
        Destroyers *John Rodgers, Stevens, Harrison, McKee, Murray*
    Destroyer Division 50
        Destroyers *Sigsbee, Ringgold, Schroeder, Dashiell*
Task Group 58.3—Rear Admiral Ted Sherman
Carrier *Essex*
    VF-83: 36 F6F-5 Hellcat
    VBF-83: 36 F4U-1D Corsair
    VB-83: 15 SB2C-4 Helldiver
    VT-83: 15 TBM-3 Avenger

Carrier *Bunker Hill*
  VF-84: 10 F6F-5 Hellcat, 27 F4U-1D Corsair
  VB-84: 15 SB2C-4 Helldiver
  VT-84: 15 TBM-3 Avenger
  VMF-221: 18 F4U-1D Corsair
  VMF-451: 18 F4U-1D Corsair
Carrier *Hancock*
  VF-6: 36 F6F-5 Hellcat
  VBF-6: 36 F6F-5 Hellcat
  VB-6: 12 SB2C Helldiver
  VT-6: 10 TBM-3 Avenger
Light carrier *Cabot*
  VF-29: 25 F6F-5 Hellcat
  VT-29: 9 TBM-3 Avenger
Light carrier *Bataan*
  VF-47: 24 F6F-5 Hellcat
  VT-47: 9 TBM-3 Avenger
Battleship Division 6 (Cooley)
  Battleships *Washington, North Carolina, South Dakota*
Cruiser Division 17 (Jones)
  Light cruisers *Pasadena, Springfield, Astoria, Wilkes-Barre*
Destroyer Squadron 62
  Destroyer Division 123
    Destroyers *Ault, English, Charles S. Sperry, Waldron, Haynsworth*
  Destroyer Division 124
    Destroyers *Wallace L. Lind, John W. Weeks, Hank, Borie*
Destroyer Squadron 48
  Destroyer Division 95
    Destroyers *Erben, Walker, Hale, Stembel*
  Destroyer Division 96
    Destroyers *Black, Bullard, Kidd, Chauncey*

Task Group 58.4—Rear Admiral Arthur Radford
Carrier *Yorktown*
  VF-9: 40 F6F-5 Hellcat
  VBF-9: 33 F6F-5 Hellcat
  VB-9: 15 SB2C-4 Helldiver
  VT-9: 7 TBM-3 Avenger
Carrier *Intrepid*
  VF-10: 6 F6F-5 Hellcat, 30 FG-1/F4U-1D Corsair
  VBF-10: 36 F4U-1D Corsair
  VB-10: 15 SB2C-4E Helldiver
  VT-10: 15 TBM-3 Avenger
Light carrier *Langley*
  VF-23: 3 F6F-3 Hellcat, 22 F6F-5 Hellcat
  VT-23. 9 TBM-1C Avenger
Light carrier *Independence*
  VF-46: 25 F6F-5 Hellcat
  VT-46: 8 TBM-3 Avenger
Battleship Division 9 (Hanson; later Denfeld)
  Battleships *Wisconsin, Missouri, New Jersey*
Cruiser Division 16 (Low)
  Large cruisers *Alaska, Guam*
  Light cruisers *St. Louis, Flint, Oakland, San Diego*
Destroyer Squadron 54
  Destroyer Division 107
    Destroyers *Remey, Norman Scott, Mertz, Monssen*
  Destroyer Division 108
    Destroyers *McGowan, McNair, Melvin*
Destroyer Squadron 47
  Destroyer Division 93
    Destroyers *McCord, Trathen, Hazelwood, Heermann*
  Destroyer Division 94
    Destroyers *Haggard, Franks, Hailey*
Destroyer Squadron 53
  Destroyer Division 105
    Destroyers *Cushing, Colahan, Uhlmann, Benham*

Task Force 51 Joint Expeditionary Force—Vice Admiral Richmond Kelly Turner (*Eldorado*) (Embarking US Tenth Army and commanding TF-52, TF-53, TF-54, and TF-55)

Task Group 51.1 Western Islands Attack Group (77th Division) —Rear Admiral Ingolf Kiland
Amphibious command ship *Mount McKinley*
Transport Group Fox
  Transport Division 49: Attack transports *Chilton, Lagrange, Tazewell, St. Mary's*, attack cargo ships *Oberon, Torrance*
  Transport Division 50: Attack transports *Henrico, Pitt, Natrona, Drew*, attack cargo ship *Tate*, ambulance transport *Rixey*
  Transport Division 51: Attack transports *Goodhue, Eastland, Telfair, Mountrail, Montrose*, attack cargo ship *Wyandot*, ambulance transport *Suffolk*
  Reconnaissance Section: Destroyer-transports *Scribner, Kinzer*
  Western Islands Tractor Flotilla: 1 LCI, 18 LST
  Western Islands Reserve Tractor Group: 10 LST
  Western Islands LSM Group: 1 LCI, 11 LSM
  Western Islands Control Unit: 3 PC, 4 SC
  Western Islands Hydrographic Survey Group: 4 PC
  Western Islands Service and Salvage Unit: ARS *Clamp*, ARL *Egeria*, fleet tugs *Yuma, Tekesta*, 2 LCI, 1 LCT
Destroyer Squadron 49
  Destroyers *Picking, Sproston, Wickes, William D. Porter, Isherwood, Kimberly, Luce, Charles J. Badger*
Escort Division 69
  Destroyer-escorts *Richard W. Suesens, Abercrombie, Oberrender, Riddle, Swearer, Stern*, destroyer-transports *Humphreys, Herbert, Dickerson,*
PCE-853
  Western Islands Pontoon Barge and Causeway Unit
    Carrying 7 pontoon causeways, 8 warping tugs, 4 pontoon barges
  10 LSTs, 18 LSTs (carrying LCTs)

Task Force 54 Gunfire and Covering Force—Rear Admiral Morton Deyo (*Tennessee*)
Battleship *Tennessee*
Unit One—Fischler
  Battleships *Texas, Maryland*
  Heavy cruiser *Tuscaloosa*
  Destroyers *Laws, Longshaw, Morrison, Prichett*
Unit Two—Joy
  Battleships *Arkansas, Colorado*
  Heavy cruisers *San Francisco, Minneapolis*
  Destroyers *Hall, Halligan, Paul Hamilton, Laffey, Twiggs*
Unit Three—Rodgers
  Battleship *Nevada*
  Heavy cruiser *Wichita*
  Light cruisers *Birmingham, St. Louis*
  Destroyers *Mannet L. Abele, Zellars, Bryant, Barton, O'Brien*
Unit Four—McCormick
  Battleships *Idaho, West Virginia*
  Heavy cruisers *Pensacola, Portland*
  Light cruiser *Biloxi*
  Destroyers *Porterfield, Callaghan, Irwin, Cassin Young, Preston*
Unit Five—Smith
  Battleships *New Mexico, New York*
  Heavy cruiser *Salt Lake City*
  Destroyers *Newcomb, Heywood, Leutze, Leary, Bennion*
Unit Six—Hinds
  Destroyer-escorts *Miles, Wesson, Foreman, Whitehurst, England, Witter, Bowers, Willmarth*

Task Force 52 Amphibious Support Force—Rear Admiral William H.P. Blandy (amphibious command ship *Estes*)
Task Group 52.1 Support Carrier Group—Rear Admiral Calvin Durgin (*Makin Island*)
Unit One—Sprague
  Escort carrier *Makin Island*
    VC-84: 16 FM-2 Wildcat, 11 TBM-3 Avenger
  Escort carrier *Fanshaw Bay*
    VOC-2: 24 FM-2 Wildcat, 6 TBM-3 Avenger

Escort carrier *Lunga Point*
VC-85: 18 FM-2 Wildcat, 11 TBM-3 Avenger,
1 TBM-3P Avenger
Escort carrier *Sangamon*
VC-85: 24 F6F Hellcat, 6 TBM-3E Avenger
Escort carrier *Natoma Bay*
VC-81: 20 FM-2 Wildcat, 11 TBM-1C Avenger,
1 TBM-1CP Avenger
Escort carrier *Savo Island*
VC-91: 20 FM-2 Wildcat, 11 TBM-1C Avenger,
4 TBM-3 Avenger
Escort carrier *Anzio*
VC-13: 12 FM-2 Wildcat, 12 TBM-1C Avenger
Destroyers *Ingraham, Patterson, Bagley, Hart, Boyd, Bradford*,
destroyer-escorts *Lawrence C. Taylor, Melvin R. Nawman,
Oliver Mitchell, Robert F. Keller, Richard M. Rowell, Richard S.
Bull, Dennis, Sederstrom, Fleming, O'Flaherty*

Unit Two—Stump
Escort carrier *Saginaw Bay*
VC-88: 20 FM-2 Wildcat, 12 TBM Avenger
Escort carrier *Sargent Bay*
VC-83: 16 FM-2 Wildcat, 12 TBM-1C Avenger
Escort carrier *Rudyerd Bay*
VC-96: 20 FM-2 Wildcat, 11 TBM-1C Avenger
Escort carrier *Marcus Island*
VC-87: 20 FM-2 Wildcat, 12 TBM-3 Avenger
Escort carrier *Tulagi*
VC-92: 19 FM-2 Wildcat, 12 TBM-3 Avenger
Escort carrier *Wake Island*
VOC-1: 26 FM-2 Wildcat, 6 TBM-3 Avenger
Destroyers *Capps, Lowry, Evans, John D. Henley*, destroyer-escorts
*William Seiverling, Ulvert M. Moore, Kendall C. Campbell,
Goss, Tisdale, Eisele*

Unit Three—Sample
Escort carrier *Suwannee*
VC-40: 17 F6F Hellcat, 10 TBM Avenger
Escort carrier *Chenango*
VC-25: 17 F6F-5 Hellcat, 1 F6F-5P Hellcat, 12 TBM Avenger
Escort carrier *Santee*
VC-24: 18 F6F Hellcat, 12 TBM Avenger
Escort carrier *Steamer Bay*
VC-90: 19 FM-2 Wildcat, 12 TBM-3 Avenger
Destroyers *Metcalf, Drexler, Fullam, Guest, Helm*
Destroyer-escorts *Edmonds, John C. Butler*
Special Escort Carrier Group
Ferrying MAG-31 (192 F4U Corsair, 30 F6F-5N Hellcat)
Escort carriers *Hollandia, White Plains, Sitkoh Bay, Breton*
Destroyer-transports *Kilty, Manley, George E. Badger, Greene*

Task Group 52.2 Mine Flotilla—Sharp (minelayer *Terror*)
Task Group 52.3 Destroyer Minesweeper Group
Unit 2: Destroyer-minesweepers *Forrest, Hobson, Macomb, Dorsey,
Hopkins, Gwin*
Unit 3: Destroyer-minesweepers *Ellyson, Hambleton, Rodman,
Emmons, Lindsey*
Unit 4: Destroyer-minesweepers *Butler, Gherardi, Jeffers, Harding,
Aaron Ward*
Task Group 52.4 Minesweeper Group One
Unit 5: Minesweepers *Champion, Heed, Defense*, destroyer-
minesweeper *Adams*, PC-584
Unit 6: Minesweepers *Requisite, Revenge, Pursuit, Sage*, destroyer-
minesweeper *Tolman*, PC-1128
Unit 7: Minesweepers *Sheldrake, Skylark, Starling, Swallow*, destroyer-
minesweeper *Henry A. Wiley*, PC-1179
Unit 8: Minesweepers *Gladiator, Impeccable, Spear, Triumph,
Vigilance*, destroyer-minesweeper *Shea*, PC-1598
Task Group 52.5 Minesweeper Group Two
Unit 9: Minesweepers *Skirmish, Staunch, Signet, Scurry, Spectacle,
Specter*, destroyer-minesweeper *Tracy*, PGM-9
Unit 10: Minesweepers *Superior, Serene, Shelter, Strategy, Strength,
Success*, destroyer-minesweeper *J. William Ditter*, PGM-10

Unit 11: Minesweepers *Ransom, Diploma, Density, Facility, Rebel,
Recruit*, PGM-11
Task group 52.6 Motor Minesweeper Group
Destroyer-minesweepers *Robert H. Smith, Shannon, Thomas E. Fraser,
Harry F. Bauer, Breese*, PGM-17, PGM-18, PGM-20, plus 7 YMS
Task group 52.7 Reserve Sweep Group
Unit 19: Minesweepers *Buoyant, Gayety, Design, Device, Hazard,
Execute*
Destroyer-transports *Reeves, Griffin, Waters, Sims*
Support Unit
Minelayer *Weehawken*, minesweeper *Monadnock*, marine
engine repair ship *Mona Island*
Task Group 52.8 Net and Buoy Group
Minelayer *Salem*, net-layers *Snowbell, Terebinth, Corkwood,
Spicewood, Cliffrose, Stagbush, Abele, Mahogany, Aloe,
Chinquapin, Winterberry, Pinon*, net-laying cargo ships *Keokuk,
Sagittarius, Tuscana*
Task Group 52.11 Underwater Demolition Flotilla
Destroyer-transport *Gilmer*
Group Able: Destroyer-transports *Bates, Barr, Bull, Knudson*
(Embarking UDT-12, -13, -14, and -19)
Group Baker: Destroyer-transports *Loy, Hopping, Kline, Raymon
W. Herndon, Crosley, Bunch*
(Embarking UDT-4, -7, -11, 16, -17, and -21)
Gunboat Support Flotilla: 36 LCI(G), 42 LCS(L), 34 LCI(R), 12 LCM(R)
Mortar Support Flotilla
Group 1: 25 LCI(M)
Group 2: 21 LCI(M)
**Task Force 53 Northern Attack Force (III Amphibious Corps)—
Rear Admiral Lawrence F. Reifsnider (*Panamint*)**
Amphibious command ship *Panamint*
Task Group 53.1 Transport Group Able (6th Marine Division)
Transport Division 34
Attack transports *Cambria, Marvin H. McIntyre, Adair, Gage,
Noble, Gilliam*
Attack cargo ships *Sheliak, Hydrus*
Transport Division 35
Attack transports *Clay, Leon, George Clymer, Arthur Middleton,
Catron*
Attack cargo ships *Caswell, Devosa*
Transport Division 36
Attack transports *Monrovia, Wayne, Sumter, Menifee, Fuller*
Attack cargo ships *Aquarius, Circe*
LSD *Casa Grande*
LSV *Catskill*
Task Group 53.2 Transport Group Baker (1st Marine Division)
Transport Division 52
Attack transports *Burleigh, McCracken, Thomas Jefferson, Charles
Carroll*
Troopship *Barnett*
Attack cargo ships *Andromeda, Cepheus*
LSD *Oak Hill*
LSV *Monitor*
Transport Division 53
Attack transports *Marathon, Rawlins, Renville, New Kent, Burleson*
Attack cargo ships *Centaurus, Arcturus*
Transport Division 54
Attack transports *Dade, Navarro, Effingham, Joseph T. Dickman*
Attack cargo ships *Betelgeuse, Procyon*
LSD *White Marsh*
Task Group 53.3 Northern Tractor Flotilla
Tractor Group Able: 15 LST, 7 LSM
Carrying 6 LCT, 22 pontoon barges, 6 pontoon causeways
Tractor Group Baker: 16 LST
Carrying 10 LCT, 16 pontoon barges, 6 pontoon causeways
Tractor Group Charlie: 14 LST, 8 LSM
Carrying 10 pontoon barges
Northern Control Group: 4 PC, 5 PCS, 9 SC

Task Group 53.6 Northern Attack Force Screen
Destroyers *Morris, Mustin, Lang, Stack, Sterett, Pringle, Hutchins,*
Massey, Russell, Wilson, Stanly, Howorth, Hugh W. Hadley, destroyer-
escorts *Gendreau, Fieberling, William C. Cole, Paul G. Baker, Bebas,*
destroyer-transports *Charles Lawrence, Roper,* 2 PCE(R), 1 SC

Task Group 53.7 Northern Defense Group
21 LST carrying LCT and pontoon causeways
Unclassified vessels *Elk* and *Camel,* destroyer-escort *Fair,* 2 SC, 7 YMS

Task Force 55 Southern Attack Force (XXIV Corps)—Rear Admiral
John L. Hall (*Teton*)

Task Group 55.1 Transport Group Dog (7th Division)
Transport Division 37
Attack transports *Harris, Lamar, Sheridan, Pierce, Tyrrell*
Attack cargo ship *Algorab*
Transport Division 38
Attack transports *Barnstable, Elmore, Alpine, Lycoming*
Attack cargo ship *Alshain*
LSD *Epping Forest*
Transport Division 39
Attack transports *Custer, Freestone, Kittson, Baxter*
Attack cargo ships *Algol, Arneb*
Transport Division 13
LSV *Ozark*
Attack transports *Appling, Butte, Audrain, Laurens*
Attack cargo ships *Aurelia, Corvus*
Tractor Group Dog: 15 LST, 12 LSM, 2 LCI
Tractor Group Fox: 14 LST, 10 LSM

Task Group 55.2 Transport Group Easy
(Embarking 96th Division)
Transport Division 40
Attack transports *Mendocino, Sarasota, Haskell, Oconto*
Attack cargo ships *Capricornus, Chara*
LSD *Lindenwald*
Transport Division 41
Attack transports *Olmsted, La Porte, Fond Du Lac, Banner*
Attack cargo ships *Diphda, Uvalde*
Transport Division 42
Attack transports *Neshoba, Oxford, Latimer, Edgecombe*
Attack cargo ship *Virgo*
LSD *Gunston Hall*
Transport Division 14
Attack transports *Allendale, Meriwether, Menard, Kenton*
Attack cargo ship *Achernar*
Tractor Group Easy: 23 LST, 5 LSM
LCS Support Division 5: 6 LCS(L)
Southern Control Party: 4 PCS, 4 PC, 7 SC
Southern Support Gunboats: 11 LCS(L), 6 LSM(R)

Task Group 55.6 Southern Attack Force Screen
Destroyers *Anthony, Bache, Bush, Mullany, Bennett, Hudson, Hyman,*
Purdy, Beale, Wadsworth, Ammen, Putnam, Rooks
Destroyer-transport *Sims*
Destroyer-escorts *Crouter, Carlson, Damon M. Cummings, Vammen,*
O'Neill, Walter C. Wann
1 PCE(R)
2 SC

Task Group 55.7 Southern Defense Group
Destroyer-escort *Manlove,* destroyer-transport *Stringham,* 34 LST, 14
LSM, six YMS, two LCI, oil storage ship *Grumium*

Task Group 55.9 Southern LCT and Pontoon Barge Group
LCT Flotillas 16–21 (60 LCT)

Task Group 50.5 Search and Reconnaissance Group
Seaplane tender *Hamlin*
VPB-208: 12 PBM-5 Mariner
Seaplane tender *St. George*
VPB-18: 12 PBM-5 Mariner
Seaplane tender *Chandeleur*
VPB-21: 12 PBM-3 Mariner
Light seaplane tenders *Yakutat, Onslow, Shelikof*
VPB-27: 12 PBM-5 Mariner
Light seaplane tender *Bering Strait*

VH-3: 6 PBM-3R Mariner
Seaplane tender destroyers *Thornton, Gillis, Williamson*

Task Group 51.2 Demonstration Group "Charlie"—Rear Admiral
Jerauld Wright
(Embarking 2nd Marine Division)
Troopship *Ancon*
Transport Squadron 15
Attack transports *Bayfield, Haskell, Hendry, Sibley, Berrien*
Attack cargo ships *Shoshone, Theenim, Southampton*
Ambulance transport *Pinkney*

Task Force 57 British Carrier Force—Vice Admiral Sir Bernard
Rawlings (*King George V*)

Task Group 57.1 First Battle Squadron—Vice Admiral Sir Bernard
Rawlings
Battleship *King George V*
Battleship *Howe*

Task Group 57.2 First Aircraft Carrier Squadron—Rear Admiral
Philip Vian
Carrier *Indomitable*: 15 Avengers, 29 Hellcats
Carrier *Victorious*: 14 Avengers, 37 Corsairs, 2 Walruses
Carrier *Illustrious*: 16 Avengers, 36 Corsairs
Carrier *Indefatigable*: 20 Avengers, 40 Seafires, 9 Fireflies
Carrier *Formidable*: 15 Avengers, 28 Corsairs

Task Group 57.4 Fourth Cruiser Squadron—Rear Admiral Eric
J.P. Brind
Light cruisers *Swiftsure, Black Prince, Euryales, Argonaut, Uganda,*
Gambia, Achilles

Task Group 57.8 Screen—Rear Admiral John H. Edelsten
24th Destroyer Flotilla
27th Destroyer Flotilla
4th Destroyer Flotilla
25th Destroyer Flotilla

TENTH ARMY TACTICAL AIR FORCE—MAJOR-GENERAL FRANCIS C. MULCAHY (USMC)

Air Defense Command
Marine Aircraft Group 43
Air Warning Squadrons 1, 6, 7, 8, and 11
Marine Aircraft Group 14
VMF-212, VMF-222, and VMF-223
Marine Aircraft Group 22
VMF-113, VMF-314, and VMF-422
VMF(N)-533
Marine Aircraft Group 31
VMF-224, VMF-311, VMF-441
VMF(N)-542
Marine Aircraft Group 33
VMF-312, VMF-322, VMF-323
VMF(N)-543

301st Fighter Wing (USAAF)
318th Fighter Group
19th, 73rd, and 333rd Fighter Squadrons
548th Night Fighter Squadron
413th Fighter Group
1st, 21st, and 34th Fighter Squadrons
507th Fighter Group
463rd, 464th, and 465th Fighter Squadrons

VII Bomber Command (USAAF)
11th Bombardment Group, Heavy
26th, 42nd, 98th, and 431st Bombardment Squadrons, Heavy
41st Bombardment Group, Medium
47th, 48th, 396th, and 820th Bombardment Squadrons, Medium
319th Bombardment Group, Light
437th, 438th, 439th, and 440th Bombardment Squadrons, Light
494th Bombardment Group, Heavy
864th, 865th, 866th, and 867th Bombardment Squadrons, Heavy
Antisubmarine Unit
VMTB-131, VMTB-232 (USMC)
Photographic Unit (TU-99.2.4)
28th Photographic Reconnaissance Squadron (USAAF)

OPPOSING PLANS

JAPANESE

IGHQ promulgated its "Outline of Army and Navy Operations" on January 20, 1945. Japan's new perimeter defense zone included Iwo Jima, Formosa, Okinawa, the south Korean coast, and the Shanghai area. The main defensive effort would be in the Ryukyus, with preparations complete by March 1945. Japanese air strength would be conserved until a US landing was underway within the defensive zone. The US invasion fleet would then be destroyed at sea "primarily by sea and air special attack units." That same day, IGHQ's Army Section published its "Outline of Air Operations in the East China Sea Area," which detailed directions for strengthening airbases, preserving and replenishing units, and redeploying airpower into the East China Sea theater by April 1.

By January 1945, IJA officers increasingly recognized that American air and naval bombardments were simply too overwhelming to resist and that aggressively meeting US forces at the water's edge was pointlessly suicidal. Instead, Japanese troops would forfeit landing beaches and deeply entrench inland in a defense-in-depth, augmented by heavily concealed and fortified artillery. There would be no brazen but foolish

Kyushu high school girls wave cherry blossoms at Second Lieutenant Toshio Anazawa, who is departing for Okinawa on a kamikaze mission, April 12, 1945. Such elaborate peer pressure was not wholly spontaneous but was a deliberately fostered part of kamikaze culture by 1945. Anazawa's Ki-43 Oscar fighter is carrying a 550lb bomb. (Public Domain)

bushido-inspired *banzai* charges of earlier years; Japanese troops would instead wage meticulous attritional war (*Jikyusen*), forcing the Americans to painfully work inland and blast the stubborn and disciplined Japanese defenders out inch-by-inch.

To provide air support to the ground troops, on February 6, 1945, IGHQ drafted a Joint Army–Navy Air Agreement to facilitate inter-service coordination:

1.   All Army and Navy air forces in the Homeland (less air defense and training forces) will be concentrated in the East China Sea area (Formosa, the Ryukyus, east China, and Korea) during the months of February and March 1945. This concentrated air strength, together with air units already in Formosa (First Air Fleet and 8th Air Division) will crush any enemy invasion attempts.

2.   Primary emphasis will be laid on the speedy activation, training, and mass employment of air special attack units.

3.   The main target of Army aircraft will be enemy transports. The main target of Navy aircraft will be carrier task forces.

This combined IJA–IJN plan was dubbed *Ten-Go* (Operation *Heaven*). Of potential US targets, IGHQ deemed Iwo Jima too minor and remote to warrant expending strength on mass air attacks. IGHQ therefore left Iwo Jima's defense to local air and ground forces, plus limited kamikaze and *Kaiten* operations. By early March however, Japanese intelligence began predicting an imminent US invasion of the far more strategic Okinawa. By March 26, IGHQ had formally subordinated IJN Third Air Fleet, Fifth Air Fleet, Tenth Air Fleet, and the IJA's Sixth Air Army under Ugaki's IJN command, temporarily unifying operational control of the Home Islands' airpower. Combined, the four Japanese air forces would mass 3,000 aircraft at Kyushu to swamp the expected US invasion in a series of coordinated mass *Kikisui* attacks. From Formosa, IJN First Air Fleet and IJA 8th Air Division contributed 300–400 additional planes.

Ten-Go's mandate ordering mass suicide attacks was not widely popular, with many Japanese officers disapproving on both tactical and moral grounds. Rear Admiral Toshiyuki Yokoi recalled, "The High Command, utterly confused by a succession of defeats, had lost all wisdom of cool judgment and had degenerated to the point of indulging in wild gambling. The order was nothing less than a national death sentence." Yokoi particularly distinguished between the limited, purely volunteer *tokko* attacks of late 1944 and the mandated mass attacks of 1945: "Once the order had been issued by Headquarters for these suicide attacks, they became, instead, 'murder attacks,' and humanity was lost sight of."

ALLIED

Spruance's US Fifth Fleet would stage Operation *Detachment* on February 19, 1945. Under Spruance's *Com5thFlt Operation Plan 13-44*, Turner's TF-51 would assault Iwo Jima with Major-General Harry Schmidt's V Amphibious Corps (VAC), comprising the 3rd and 4th Marine Divisions with 5th Marine Division in reserve. Spruance planned three days of pre-invasion air–sea bombardment against Iwo Jima, beginning on February 16 (D-3). Simultaneously, Mitscher's TF-58 would screen TF-51 with several days of preemptive airstrikes against Tokyo-area airfields. TF-58 would then return to directly support *Detachment*'s February 19 D-Day, before retiring to Ulithi to prepare for *Iceberg*. Direct air support at Iwo Jima would be provided by the ten escort carriers of Rear Admiral Calvin Durgin's Support Carrier Group (TG-52.2). US planners expected to have Iwo Jima's three airfields operational by D+7, D+10, and D+50, allowing defense responsibilities to pass to the Iwo Jima-based VII Fighter Command.

Marines unload an LCI flotilla in Iwo Jima's high surf during Operation *Detachment*. In 1944, the US Pacific Fleet's amphibious mastermind, Vice Admiral Richmond Kelly Turner, even suggested bypassing everything and landing nine US divisions directly onto the Tokyo plain. The concept was technically feasible, although highly risky without land-based air support. (US Coast Guard)

Spruance's staff planned *Detachment* and *Iceberg* simultaneously. Okinawa's *Iceberg* therefore received an "L-Day" designation to avoid confusion with *Detachment*'s more standard "D-Day." *Iceberg* planners expected "that Iwo Jima [would be] seized at a sufficiently early date to permit the gun support and air support units to participate in the assault on Okinawa [and that] assault shipping and supporting naval forces would [be] released from the Luzon operations."

Spruance outlined his *Iceberg* strategy in *Com5thFlt Operation Plan 1-45*. Beginning on March 18 (L-14), Mitscher's TF-58 fast carriers would launch preemptive strikes against Japanese airpower in Kyushu. Then on March 25 (L-7), TF-58 and TF-51 air and fire support units would converge off Okinawa to commence seven days' air and naval pre-invasion bombardment. Finally, on Easter Sunday, April 1 (L-Day), US Tenth Army's III Amphibious Corps and XXIV Corps would land four assault divisions 11 miles north of Naha on southwestern Okinawa's Hagushi beaches, where the Kadena and Yontan airfields lay just 2,000yds inland. Upon Kadena's and Yontan's capture, the ground-based TAF would be established ashore as rapidly as possible.

Until then, Mitscher's hard-pressed fast carriers (TF-58) would have to simultaneously suppress Kyushu and Ryukyus airfields, provide the invasion fleet's main air defense, provide close air support (CAS) for Tenth Army ashore, and of course defend itself. Such missions would tie TF-58 to a stationary area off Okinawa, surrounded by and within easy range (340–360nm) of Kyushu (55 airfields), Formosa (65 airfields), and the China coast. Additional Japanese airfields existed 150nm away in the Amami Gunto and 230nm away in the Sakishima Gunto. To prosecute *Iceberg*, US forces would need to sustain enormous combat, support, and logistic operations deep within enemy waters—Okinawa lay 900nm (four days' steaming time) from Leyte; 1,200nm (five days) from Ulithi or Guam; 4,040nm (17 days) from Pearl Harbor; and 6,200nm (26 days) from the US West Coast.

THE CAMPAIGN

COMMENCING *DETACHMENT*, FEBRUARY 16–20, 1945

Iwo Jima and the Nanpo Shoto
Iwo Jima belongs to the Nanpo Shoto island chain, which extends 750nm south from Honshu towards the Marianas. The Nanpo Shoto is divided into three groups, with the Izut Shoto (including Hachijo Jima) in the north, the Bonin Islands (including Chichi Jima and Haha Jima) in the center, and finally the Volcano Islands (Kazan Retto) in the south.

Iwo Jima lies 650nm south of Tokyo in the Volcano Islands. At just 8.1 square miles, Iwo Jima is barely one-third the size of New York's Manhattan Island. The volcanically active rock reeks of sulfur (Iwo Jima means "Sulfur Island") and its hot surface is riven with fumaroles belching noxious smoke from beneath. Unusually fine volcanic ash and cinders comprise Iwo Jima's black beaches. Dominating the small island in its extreme southwest is the 554ft ASL Mount Suribachi volcano. By early 1945 the Japanese had two double-strip airfields operational, with a third under construction. All civilians had been evacuated.

Defending Iwo Jima were 20,933 Japanese troops (13,586 IJA soldiers and 7,347 armed IJN personnel) commanded by the brilliant defensive tactician Lieutenant-General Tadamichi Kuribiyashi. The Japanese garrison was fully subterranean and comprised 5,000 skillfully concealed cave entrances and pillboxes. Within these hidden underground fortifications were 361 artillery pieces, 77 mortars, 33 large-caliber coastal defense guns, nearly 300 antiaircraft guns, 69 antitank guns, 70 rocket launchers, and 24 tanks.

Some 120nm north of Iwo Jima, in the Bonins, mountainous Haha Jima was too rugged for a major airfield. Boasting two excellent harbors, it was defended by 7,000 Japanese troops. Thirty miles farther north and 150nm north of Iwo Jima was the equally rugged Chichi Jima, which had an airstrip and a large harbor. Chichi Jima was heavily fortified by 14,000 Japanese troops and many antiaircraft guns.

Detachment pre-landing operations, February 16–18
Fifth Fleet's pre-landing naval bombardment of Iwo Jima proved one of the most bitter and enduring controversies of the Pacific War. The marines

had insisted on ten days' shelling, but Spruance only allotted three. A ten day-long bombardment, Spruance reasoned, would destroy operational surprise and was logistically untenable anyway. Additionally, when considering Iwo's hardened, concealed emplacements, a ten-day shelling would have far exceeded the point of decreasing returns. Writing from Iwo Jima in March 1945, *TIME* magazine correspondent Robert Sherrod would claim: "At Iwo the Japs dug themselves in so deeply that all the explosives in the world could hardly have reached them."

Indeed, Iwo had already been heavily bombarded. Between August 10, 1944 and February 15, 1945 (D-4), US forces had pounded Iwo Jima with 9,616 tons of aerial and naval munitions. Of this total, 5,582 tons had been delivered by B-24s, 1,223 tons by B-29s, and 406 tons by USN aircraft. Four USN battleship and cruiser bombardments accounted

B-24 Liberators bomb Iwo Jima in late 1944. Lieutenant-General Holland M. Smith (USMC) nevertheless reported: "The prolonged aerial bombardment of Iwo Jima, which was a daily occurrence for over 70 days, had no appreciable effect in the reduction of the enemy's well-prepared and heavily-fortified defensive installations." A Japanese POW later reported that at least 40 percent of bombs dropped by USAAF bombers missed the island completely. (NHHC NH 65318)

for the remaining 2,405 tons. After the initial pre-landing naval shelling began on February 16 (D-3), USN warships expended another 9,907 tons of ordnance, with B-24s adding 127 tons of bombs. By D-Day, February 19, the Americans had already plastered Iwo with over 2,425 tons of projectiles per square mile. This comes to 3.79 tons of munitions per acre, or nearly three tons of bombs and shells per American football field over the entire island.

Turner's TF-51 comprised 495 warships, transports, and support ships to land, support, and sustain two assault divisions and one reserve division at Iwo Jima. Within the Attack Force (TF-53) were 43 attack transports, 16 attack cargo ships, 63 LSTs, 58 LCIs, and 18 LCI(G) gunboats. Aboard the Attack Force was V Amphibious Corps comprising the 3rd, 4th, and 5th Marine Divisions and attached units, totaling 80,618 personnel and 84,790 tons of supplies and equipment, including 7,311 vehicles, plus the USAAF 15th Fighter Group.

Rodgers' hastily improvised bombardment force comprised the ancient battleships *Idaho*, *Tennessee*, *Nevada*, *Texas*, *Arkansas*, and *New York*; heavy cruisers *Chester*, *Pensacola*, *Salt Lake City*, and *Tuscaloosa*; light cruiser *Vicksburg*; and 16 destroyers. *Nevada*, *Texas*, *Arkansas*, and *Tuscaloosa* had all recently reached the Pacific from Operations *Overlord* and *Dragoon*, while *New York* was seeing her first amphibious action since Operation *Torch*. Spruance additionally promised Turner the 16in.-gunned fast battleships *North Carolina* and *Washington* by D-Day.

Accompanied by Spruance in *Indianapolis*, Mitscher's TF-58 opened heavy airfield suppression strikes against the Tokyo area the morning of February 16 (D-3). Meanwhile, 650nm to the south, Blandy's TF-52 (Amphibious Support Force) and Rodgers' TF-54 (Gunfire and Covering Force) arrived off a misty, rainy Iwo Jima. Despite the poor visibility, TF-52 and TF-54 commenced *Detachment*'s pre-landing naval bombardment at 0800hrs.

Kuribiyashi had skillfully developed Iwo's fixed defenses. A multitude of intricate, heavily protected, and interconnected but independent small strongpoints were widely dispersed, localizing potential bomb damage. Kuribiyashi kept his flak positions concealed and made his coastal guns count by seldom firing unless they had a good target. Even then, Japanese powder

Flying over Iwo from west to east, four TBM Avengers bomb Japanese positions in southern Iwo Jima, between South Field and Central Field. At the bottom the East Boat Basin is visible beneath the Quarry cliffs. Suribachi is out of frame to the left. (Corbis via Getty Images)

The Iwo Jima shoreline being pounded by white phosphorous, February 17, 1945. This was a covering bombardment for the UDT mission to destroy underwater obstacles. Despite US efforts, previously unknown Japanese coast artillery batteries devastated the LCI gunboats covering the frogmen, inflicting heavy casualties. (NHHC NH 104337-KN)

produced frustratingly little flash and smoke. Mortars, antitank guns, and inactive guns remained hidden until they could be used to advantage. US officers openly credited the Japanese with "unusual and painstaking concealment of vital defenses and gun positions" undetectable by eye or camera lens, largely negating US photoreconnaissance. Guns emplaced in caves proved exceedingly difficult to destroy even when discovered.

Rear Admiral Calvin Durgin's Support Carrier Group (TG-52.2) of ten escort carriers, seven destroyers, and six destroyer-escorts mounted 239 sorties on February 16, but poor weather aborted a raid by 42 B-24s. An amusing incident that afternoon saw a *Pensacola* OS2U Kingfisher floatplane dogfight and splash a Zero that had apparently scrambled from Iwo. US aircraft strafed and destroyed another three G4M Betties on the ground. Iwo Jima's antiaircraft fire was reportedly "hot and heavy" for the first few days, but few US aircraft would be shot down.

However, observation of February 16's medium-range gunfire revealed little apparent damage. US officers conceded, "Against such defenses, long- or medium-range gunfire simply is not effective, and a tremendous amount of valuable ammunition can be wasted in general area fire."

February 17 saw much clearer weather. At 0641hrs, three G4M Betties attacked radar picket destroyer *Halligan* (DD-584) 20nm north of Iwo Jima but were repulsed with one Betty shot down. Japanese aerial opposition otherwise remained light. After February 16's disappointing results, Rodgers' battleships and cruisers closed within 1,800yds to hammer Japanese guns, pillboxes, and blockhouses along the shore. A later USN report explained, "The hard unpleasant fact must be acknowledged that direct hits must be scored repeatedly. This necessitates close point-blank ranges and acute observation" and acknowledged that "the risk of enemy hits may have to be accepted to do the job."

Between 0911hrs and 1025hrs battleships *Idaho*, *Nevada*, and *Tennessee* slung heavy direct fire into Japanese targets. Coastal artillery would lightly damage *Tennessee*, but at 0935hrs Japanese 4.7in. and 6in. shore batteries suddenly hit cruiser *Pensacola* six times, killing 17 (including her executive officer) and wounding 98. *Pensacola* temporarily withdrew before returning to complete her fire support mission.

At 1100hrs, destroyer-transports *Bull* (APD-78), *Barr* (APD-39), *Bates* (APD-47), and *Blessman* (APD-48) launched LCP(R)s carrying over 100 UDT frogmen to reconnoiter and demolish underwater obstacles. Covering the LCP(R)s were rocket-firing LCI(G)s. However, previously undiscovered Japanese coast artillery suddenly erupted, hitting all 12 LCI(G)s, sinking *LCI(G)-474*, and ultimately killing 37 Americans and wounding 144. Covering destroyer *Leutze* (DD-481) was also hit, severely wounding four men, including her skipper. *Leutze* remained in action, her command devolving permanently onto 27-year-old Lieutenant Leon Grabowsky.

Meanwhile, battleship *Nevada* began shelling the revealed Japanese batteries at point-blank range, eventually suppressing them after two hours. At 1330hrs, the US ships suspended their bombardment while 42 B-24s bombed Suribachi's northern slope with 260lb frag clusters from 5,000ft. Nevertheless, after two days of pre-landing bombardments, US officers considered the results so far disappointing, admitting that "relatively little destruction had been accomplished."

By morning February 18, TF-58 was returning from its Tokyo raid, having launched 2,415 combined daylight sorties on February 16–17. Clark's TG-58.1 and Radford's TG-58.4 then launched fighter sweeps and small strikes against Japanese picket boats, installations, and shipping at Haha Jima and Chichi Jima; they were joined by Durgin's escort carriers, which sank gunboat *No. 2 Hiyashi Maru* at Chichi Jima. As planned, Mitscher dispatched fast battleships *North Carolina* and *Washington*, light cruisers *Santa Fe* and *Biloxi*, and a destroyer division to reinforce Rodgers' TF-54; Spruance accompanied them aboard *Indianapolis*.

Rodgers' battleships now closed within 1,500yds of Iwo. Even the ships' 40mm antiaircraft guns were trained onto caves, machine gun nests, and light artillery; a *Nevada* 40mm battery had the satisfaction of cutting down six Japanese troops fleeing a damaged bunker. Despite low clouds and sporadic rain, Durgin's escort carriers flew 318 sorties on February 18, but the scheduled B-24s again had to abort. Meanwhile, north-northwest of Iwo Jima, Japanese bombers damaged TF-51's destroyer-minelayer *Gamble* (DM-15) and destroyer-transport *Blessman* (APD-48), killing 47 and wounding 38.

D-Day, February 19

Embarked 8,000yds offshore in 24 LSTs were eight marine Battalion Landing Teams (BLT). Six BLTs would land abreast across a two-mile, six-battalion stretch on Iwo's southeast shore, between Mount Suribachi in Iwo's extreme southwest and the East Boat Basin to the northeast. The seventh and eighth BLTs reinforced each flank. D-Day's schedule called for 9,000 marines ashore in the first 45 minutes. Turner assigned each BLT its own destroyer for direct gunfire support.

Seven battleships, four heavy cruisers, three light cruisers, and ten destroyers opened a deliberate D-Day bombardment at 0640hrs. The naval shelling paused at 0805hrs so that 120 TF-58 planes could strafe and rocket the landing zone. Meanwhile, 15 B-24s dumped 19 tons of 100lb bombs on Iwo's eastern beaches from 4,000ft. The naval barrage resumed at "vastly increased tempo" at 0825hrs, climaxing with the heaviest pre-H-Hour bombardment to date.

At 0830hrs, Turner ordered the initial wave ashore. From the Line of Departure 4,000yds offshore, the 4kt LVTs needed 30 minutes to make landfall. During this period US warships hit the landing beaches with 8,000 shells. At 0857hrs the naval shelling transferred from the shoreline to the beaches' flanks and rear. Three minutes later the first assault wave of

Battleship *Nevada* bombards Iwo on D-Day, February 19. Rear Admiral B.J. Rodgers' Gunfire and Covering Force (TF-54) was to have included seven slow battleships: *Texas, Nevada, New Mexico, Mississippi, California, Colorado,* and *West Virginia*. However, *New Mexico, Mississippi,* and *California* had taken kamikaze hits at Lingayen Gulf, while *Colorado* had been damaged by friendly fire. All four required repairs and would miss *Detachment*. Still needed off Lingayen, *West Virginia* would also miss the pre-landing bombardment. (NARA via Mighty90)

Carrying marine assault troops, a flotilla of LVTs heads for Iwo Jima the morning of D-Day, February 19, 1945. Weather conditions were ideal for landings, with calm seas, a 7kt breeze, and unlimited visibility. Within days the weather would again turn sour. (NHHC NH 104317-KN)

68 howitzer-armed LVT(A) amtanks landed on time at 0900hrs, then drove inland 50yds behind a rolling barrage of naval secondary batteries. The subsequent second through fifth LVT waves landed assault troops. LCMs and LCVPs comprised Wave 6, with Sherman tanks arriving in the LCTs and LSMs of Wave 6A.

Iwo's steep beach broke surf in 4ft breakers directly at the shoreline. The relentless heavy swells inevitably caused boats to broach and many eventually swamped and foundered. Landing craft wreckage began to pile up at the beaches and then seawards. Sherman tank-carrying LSTs and LSMs began landing at 0944hrs, but these too struggled against surf and beach conditions. Tanks that successfully landed often threw their treads once they tried to maneuver on the soft sand. Finally, the marines were pinned down at surf's edge, as penetration inland was badly stymied by three 15ft-tall, 45-degree natural terraces at the back of the beaches.

D-Day nevertheless saw a slow, bloody consolidation of the beachhead. Meanwhile, at 1045hrs the old battleship *West Virginia* suddenly arrived off Iwo and reported to Rodgers. She had steamed 900nm on just a few hours' notice, having departed Ulithi at daybreak February 16. By 1300hrs *West Virginia* was engaging Japanese targets ashore. By D-Day's end, all 4th and 5th Marine Division BLTs had been landed, along with half of the marines' divisional artillery. Total US personnel ashore came to 30,000. Throughout *Detachment* US destroyers would lob starshells all night to thwart Japanese infiltration attempts.

On February 20 (D+1), TF-58 and TG-52.2 carriers combined for 545 sorties against Iwo Jima, expending 116 tons of bombs and 1,331 rockets. Mitscher's fast carriers also launched morning and afternoon fighter sweeps against Haha Jima and Chichi Jima. However, it was Durgin's TG-52.2 escort carriers, operating 30nm off Iwo Jima, which would provide most of the marines' aerial observation and CAS. Marines ashore would request 188 CAS missions throughout the unexpectedly long, 36-day Iwo Jima battle. Of these a third were accomplished within 15 minutes of the call, and two-thirds within 30 minutes.

Winds had increased to 14–20kts on D+1, and by D+3 it would be raining hard and gusting over 25kts. In the contested shipping off Iwo, multiple US ships a day would suffer damage from friendly fire, collisions, heavy weather, and/or operational accidents. Unlucky *LST-928* would suffer nine collisions with eight different ships during *Detachment*, while attack transport *Logan* (APA-196) would ram and hole sister ship *Napa* (APA-157), requiring *Napa's* withdrawal for major repairs. The Americans would clear most landing craft wreckage by D+7 and further decongest beaches by constructing Marston matting-covered beach exits inland. However, poor sea conditions still limited landings to LSTs, LSMs, and LCTs.

KAMIKAZE ATTACKS AGAINST FIFTH FLEET, FEBRUARY 21

On February 21, Vice Admiral Teraoka's Third Air Fleet launched the only significant aerial counterattack against *Detachment*. At 0800hrs, Lieutenant Hiroshi Murakawa's *Mitate* Unit No. 2 departed Yokosuka's Katori airfield comprising 12 D4Y Judy bombers, eight B6N Jill bombers, and 12 A6M Zero escorts. After landing and refueling at Hachijo Jima, they continued towards Iwo.

Mitscher's TF-58 had repulsed 18–20 Japanese planes overnight, splashing two. As day broke TF-58 struck both Iwo Jima and Chichi Jima. Mitscher then detached Captain L.A. Moebus' fast night carrier *Saratoga*, large cruiser *Alaska*, and three destroyers to Durgin's TG-52.2 to provide night cover to the Iwo Jima assault fleet. *Saratoga* had barely reached her station 30nm northeast of Iwo Jima when, at 1628hrs, US radar detected incoming bogies.

Saratoga's CAP shot down two attackers, but at 1659hrs, six Japanese aircraft suddenly appeared out of the overcast and dove on the big carrier. *Saratoga*'s antiaircraft fire splashed one, but two low-level attackers flew into *Saratoga*'s side, their bombs detonating deep within her hull. The fourth dropped a bomb that detonated on *Saratoga*'s anchor windlass. The fifth plane slammed into *Saratoga*'s port catapult, and a final plane crashed into an aircraft crane, sending a flaming wing into Gallery No. 1. The entire attack had taken three minutes.

Then at 1846hrs three more kamikazes attacked *Saratoga*. Her escorting large cruiser *Alaska* emitted "such a barrage that she appeared to be in flames herself." Two kamikazes were shot down, but the third dropped a bomb, then immediately crashed into *Saratoga*. The kamikaze itself ricocheted over *Saratoga*'s side, doing little harm, but the bomb penetrated the hangar, causing heavy damage and blowing a 25ft-wide hole in *Saratoga*'s flight deck.

By 2015hrs *Saratoga* was again able to recover aircraft, although not launch them. In the fading light she landed five of her own Hellcats, plus a *Makin Island* Wildcat. Seemingly unaware of his location, the Wildcat pilot climbed out of his fighter and remarked to a deckhand, "Gee, I'm glad I'm not on the old *Sara*. All hell's broken loose out there!" Nonplussed, the airdale retorted, "Take a good look around, brother. This *is* hell!"

Although heavily damaged, *Saratoga* was still underway. She had suffered 123 killed and missing and another 192 wounded. *Saratoga* lost a total of 42 planes: 36 to damage aboard, and another six to ditchings. The aging, battered

US sailors fight fires aboard *Saratoga* during the February 21, 1945 attack. With a turning radius of 1,290yds, the 974ft, 36,000-ton *Saratoga* was the least maneuverable ship in the US Navy. She was repaired after *Detachment* but relegated to permanent training duty at Pearl Harbor. (Public Domain)

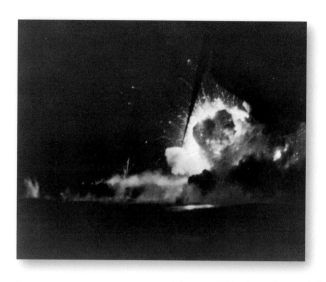

Escort carrier *Bismarck Sea* (CVE-95) explodes the night of February 21/22, 1945 as viewed from *Saginaw Bay*. To one *Saginaw Bay* sailor, the blazing *Bismarck Sea* and *Lunga Point* resembled "Broadway and 42nd Street on New Year's Eve." *Bismarck Sea* was arguably the most significant US warship sunk during *Detachment* or *Iceberg*. (NHHC 80-G-335103)

Saratoga duly retired for repairs; she never saw front-line service again.

Twenty minutes after first hitting *Saratoga*, several of Murakawa's kamikazes attacked a formation of net tenders and LSTs some 50nm southeast of Iwo Jima. One slammed into net cargo ship *Keokuk* (AKN-4), killing 17 and wounding 44, while a second kamikaze bounced harmlessly off *LST-477*.

Cruising 35nm south of *Saratoga* and 30nm east of Iwo were TG-52.2 escort carriers. Suddenly at 1845hrs, six B6N Jills roared low over the water towards escort carrier *Lunga Point* (CVE-94) and the Task Units erupted with antiaircraft fire. The first three Jills launched two torpedoes that missed, with two Jills shot down. The fourth Jill's torpedo also just missed, but hit by antiaircraft fire, the Jill dove into *Lunga Point* and exploded. *Lunga Point* suffered heavy fire damage but remained on station.

Simultaneously, a seventh Jill attacked escort carrier *Bismarck Sea* (CVE-95) from an altitude of 25ft. Despite absorbing brilliant tracers, the Jill slammed into *Bismarck Sea*'s side, destroying an elevator, starting fires, and knocking torpedoes loose. Then just two minutes later a second kamikaze "came out of nowhere" and dove into *Bismarck Sea* and exploded. Secondary explosions begun erupting from hot ordnance, and at 1905hrs the order was given to abandon ship. Moments later *Bismarck Sea* was rocked by a huge explosion, probably a torpedo detonating. The battered escort carrier capsized at 2007hrs and slid under the waves eight minutes later, having lost 218 men out of 943. *Bismarck Sea* remains the last US carrier sunk at sea by enemy action.

WINNING IWO JIMA, FEBRUARY 24–MARCH 26

To replace *Saratoga*, fast night carrier *Enterprise* formally joined Durgin's TG-52.2 at 0600hrs, February 24; the irreverent escort carrier sailors inevitably nicknamed her "*Enterprise Bay*" and "Queen of the Jeeps." From February 23 through March 2, *Enterprise* would conduct 174 straight hours of flight operations until interrupted for 45 minutes by bad weather.

Meanwhile, Mitscher's TF-58 struck Tokyo again on February 25. TF-58's combined February 16–25 attacks had delivered 378 tons of bombs in 2,471 sorties against the Tokyo area, having substantially damaged four major aircraft factories and shot up 23 airfields. Total US air losses were 88 aircraft and 63 aircrew. TF-58 flyers claimed a highly dubious 611 Japanese aircraft destroyed. Additionally, TF-58 had unknowingly wrecked planned *Ohka* missions against *Detachment* when Konioke airfield strikes destroyed all 24 modified Betty motherships.

On March 1, while returning from the Tokyo strikes, TF-58 would pound Okinawa, including shipping. TF-58 planes additionally blanketed Okinawa with excellent photographic reconnaissance coverage vital for the upcoming *Iceberg*. Hours later, in the early dark of March 2, the detached

The Battle of Iwo Jima, February 24–March 26, 1945

Kitano Point

Kangoku
Iwa

Hanare Iwa

Mar 11

Hill 371

Nishi

North
Field

Mar 1

Hill
362

Moto
Yama

Hill 354

Hill 382

Central
Field

Feb 24

Tachiwa
Point

Mar 11

XX
3 Mar

South
Field

Feb 19

XX
4 Mar

Feb 19

Suribachi
Yama

XX
5 Mar

Tobiishi
hana

N

Area of last Japanese resistance

0   1 mile

0   1km

A TBM Avenger on a close air support (CAS) mission over Iwo Jima, February 24, 1945. Marines have dug into the sand for cover. Suribachi looms in the background. For reasons never discovered, over half the napalm bombs expended against Iwo Jima proved to be duds. (USMC via Mighty90)

TF-58 light cruisers *Vincennes, Miami, San Diego,* and eight destroyers would bombard a reported radar station at Okino Daito Jima in the Ryukyus before returning to TG-58.1. Simultaneously, destroyers of TG-58.3's DesDiv-109 shelled Japanese facilities at Parece Vela (Douglas Reef). TF-58 then retired to Ulithi to prepare for *Iceberg.*

Meanwhile, the IJN had immediately deployed the *Chihaya* group of *Kaiten*-armed submarines to attack US shipping at Iwo. By February 26, the Americans had already repulsed *I-44*, while *I-368* was sunk 35nm west of Iwo Jima by Avengers of escort carrier *Anzio* (CVE-57). *Anzio* also sank submarine *RO-43* some 50nm west-northwest of Iwo Jima. Meanwhile, 120nm south of Iwo Jima, destroyer-escort *Finnegan* (DE-307) sank a third *Chihaya* submarine, *I-370.*

On February 27, Japanese shore batteries and mortar fire damaged attack cargo ship *Leo* (AKA-60), *LST-884,* and *LSM-92,* while a Japanese bomber damaged destroyer *Bennett* (DD-473). That same day, the first of 15 PBM Mariners and three "Dumbo" PB2Y Seacats would arrive to conduct search-and-rescue missions. Employing jet-assisted take-off, they would operate from Iwo's shallow waters surrounding Suribachi.

Japanese coastal artillery remained defiant. On March 1, hours after evading a Japanese air-dropped torpedo, destroyer *Terry* (DD-513) found herself dueling an Iwo shore battery. Before silencing it, *Terry* had suffered 11 dead and 19 wounded to a 6in. hit. Additionally, off northeastern Iwo Jima, an 80mm battery struck destroyer *Colhoun* (DD-801), killing one and wounding 16. Meanwhile, ammunition ship *Columbia Victory* found herself closely bracketed by Japanese artillery fire while she was approaching western Iwo Jima. To avoid obliterating half the island, she retreated offshore, miraculously without getting hit. However, Japanese coastal artillery damaged light cruiser *Biloxi,* while destroyer *Bennett* (DD-473) weathered a dud torpedo or bomb.

The unexpectedly grueling land battle had slowly begun to favor the Americans, with the marines taking Central Field on March 1. By March 3, all US assault shipping had successfully unloaded and begun withdrawing from Iwo Jima. Between February 19 (D-Day) and March 3 (D+12), marine casualties had averaged 1,034 a day. But on March 4, casualties fell to 204, and would average 322 per day thereafter.

Developing Iwo Jima airpower
Landing on D-Day was Commander R.C. Johnson's 9th Naval Construction (Seabee) Brigade, comprised of the 8th and 41st Naval Construction Regiments and the USAAF's 811th Engineer Aviation Battalion. They began immediate US airfield construction. On February 24, covered by marine rifles and shelled by Japanese artillery, the Seabees had begun crawling across South Field to remove landmines and airstrip debris. Two days later, the marines' first L-5 spotter planes began landing and by February 28, South Field began receiving crippled carrier aircraft. By then the USAAF

9th Troop Carrier Squadron had already airdropped 4.5 tons of supplies near Iwo's western beaches. Three days later drops shifted to South Field; these included 81mm mortar rounds, medical supplies, radio gear, and mail.

The first USMC transport, a Curtiss R5C (naval C-46 Commando), would land at South Field from Guam on March 4 and unload 2.75 tons of munitions. That same day, the very first B-29 Superfortress, the damaged *Dinah Might*, would emergency land at South Field to marine cheers. Iwo's second airfield, Central Field, would be operational March 16, with one strip 5,200ft and the other 4,800ft.

Led by Brigadier-General Ernest M. Moore, the 15th Fighter Group's 47th Fighter Squadron (27 P-51D Mustangs) landed at Iwo Jima's South Field on March 6, accompanied by 12 P-61D Black Widows of the 548th Night Fighter Squadron. Over the coming weeks, Moore's full strength (the 15th, 21st, and 506th Fighter Groups) would accumulate at Iwo Jima and begin combat operations. Meanwhile, the first Tinian-based PB4Y Privateers (USN B-24s) began using Iwo Jima's South Field as a staging base to increase their search range by an additional 1,200nm.

On March 7, P-51s of the 45th and 78th Fighter Squadrons reached Iwo from Saipan, allowing air support against Iwo Jima targets to transition to Iwo-based aircraft. The 15th Fighter Group began daily dawn-till-dusk CAP flights of 12 P-51s each, with two P-61s taking over at night. With little Japanese-occupied territory remaining to shell, most of TF-54 retired to Ulithi. Cruisers *Salt Lake City* and *Tuscaloosa*, and several destroyers would remain another five days before also withdrawing. By March 8, three PBY5A Landcats began operating out of South Field, replacing the PB2Ys in the "Dumbo" role. Iwo Jima's seaplanes and tenders returned to Saipan. That same day, US escort carriers began withdrawing from Iwo Jima.

P-61s flew Iwo Jima's first night intercept against two radar-detected bogies late on March 8. Relieved of her night responsibilities, *Enterprise* retired to Ulithi. Beginning on March 10, daily eight-plane flights of 15th Fighter Group P-51s began remaining on station between 0700hrs and 1830hrs for CAS calls. Quickly learning on the job, Iwo-based P-51s strafed and bombed Japanese bunkers, trenches, gun emplacements, and cave entrances, ultimately flying 125 CAS missions during *Detachment*. All the while, 15th Fighter Group's South Field fell under occasional Japanese artillery fire.

On March 11 the 47th Fighter Squadron's Colonel Jim Beckwith led 17 P-51s from South Field to bomb Chichi Jima. With Brigadier-General Moore along in his own P-51 to observe, Beckwith's Mustangs dumped a total of 24 500lb bombs on Chichi Jima's Susaki airfield, scoring 22 hits. P-51s of the 45th Fighter Squadron would hit Haha Jima the

The first Marine L-5 observation plane lands at Iwo's South Field, February 26, 1945. At Iwo, *LST-776* debuted the Brodie Sea Rig, which allowed 6–10 light observation planes to be carried, launched, and theoretically recovered aboard. A total of 20 L-5 artillery observation planes would be brought to Iwo Jima for VMO-4 and VMO-5: six aboard *LST-776* and 14 aboard seven escort carriers. (USMC)

Colonel Jim Beckwith, commander 15th Fighter Group, leads P-51 Mustangs of the 45th and 78th Fighter Squadrons to Iwo Jima, March 7, 1945. Beckwith is flying *Squirt*, the P-51 in the far upper-left. Joining the P-51s at Iwo would be P-61 night fighters. (USAAF via WW2DB)

THE USAAF 47TH FIGHTER SQUADRON STRIKES CHICHI JIMA, MARCH 11, 1945 (PP.32–33)

At 0900hrs, March 11, 17 P-51D Mustangs (**1**) took off from Iwo Jima's South Field. They were led by 15th Fighter Group commander Colonel Jim Beckwith. Fifteen P-51s were from the 47th Fighter Squadron. Along with Beckwith, they carried two 500lb bombs each. Flying along to observe was the VII Fighter Command skipper, Brigadier-General Ernest Moore, who flew the seventeenth and last P-51. A US Navy PBY Catalina, already aloft, was assigned for potential air–sea rescue.

The March 11, 1945 raid was the first US airstrike against Chichi Jima originating from Iwo Jima. Mountainous Chichi Jima had a single small airstrip, Susaki airfield (**2**). Susaki no longer hosted Japanese fighters, but the island itself was occupied by 14,000 Japanese troops and defended with heavy numbers of anti-aircraft batteries.

Upon reaching Chichi Jima, Brigadier-General Moore, callsign "Chieftain One," began orbiting about a mile southwest of Susaki airfield to observe the attack. Meanwhile Colonel Beckwith, callsign "Invader One," led his remaining 16 Mustangs to an attack position southeast of Susaki, so the Americans could attack out of the sun. Beckwith, directly leading the four Mustangs of Red Flight, opened the attack by pushing over into his dive at an

altitude of 10,000ft. Four Japanese aircraft (**3**) were parked on the runway. Red Flight released its eight bombs at 4,000ft, aiming for two of the Japanese planes. Six bombs hit the target area. Susaki field antiaircraft guns opened fire, causing black puffs of flak to begin blossoming from 2,000ft. Red Flight recovered from its dive by strafing the remaining two aircraft on the field, then headed out to the harbor to await the following P-51s' dives. The remaining flights followed in a diving attack on Susaki airfield. However, with Susaki now heavily obscured by smoke and dust, the Americans' last element, Yellow Flight, was unable to pick out any targets. It instead bombed the small craft sheltering in Chichi Jima's harbor.

Beckwith then led his charges south to nearby Haha Jima. At 1030hrs, from an altitude of 4,000ft, the P-51s began diving strafing runs across the Haha Jima town of Kitmura, before strafing a weather station and warehouse at the nearby town of Okimura. Two P-51s were damaged, but none were shot down. Having successfully struck his assigned targets, Beckwith led his Mustangs back to Iwo Jima. No P-51s had been lost. The VII Fighter Command's first offensive mission from Iwo Jima had been an unqualified success.

following day, and 78th Fighter Squadron struck Chichi Jima on March 13. From then on, weather permitting, Iwo Jima-based P-51s would strike the Bonins daily, with P-61s flying nightly harassment raids from March 29 through April 20. Some 1,638 sorties would be flown against the Bonins by war's end, with only two planes lost to combat and eight operationally.

When flying CAS at Iwo Jima, Moore's P-51s often bombed and strafed Japanese positions mere hundreds of yards from their own airstrip. With such support, the methodically advancing marines would permanently silence Iwo's Japanese artillery and mortar fire by March 13. Resistance ashore was now just small arms. The following day, Moore's P-51s flew their last CAS missions.

A TBM-3 Avenger over Iwo Jima, March 1945. Within days of the invasion, Iwo had become overrun with flies feeding on the thousands of bodies. On February 28, escort carrier *Makin Island* responded with an Avenger flight that sprayed DDT pesticide over the island. The experiment proved so successful that it was repeated on March 4 and added to *Iceberg* plans. (NHHC 80-G-412474)

The marines suffered just 149 casualties on March 23, followed by none on March 24–25, suggesting that Iwo might be conquered. But then at 0400hrs, March 26, some 350 Japanese erupted seemingly from nowhere and charged Central Field, attacking stunned US sentries with swords and small arms before slitting through tents to throw grenades at trapped, just-woken Americans inside. Startled US airmen fought back with pistols and carbines, while African-American labor troops and the Marine 5th Pioneer Battalion, housed nearby, promptly counterattacked the bivouac.

The shocked Americans inevitably began to rally. As dawn broke, an improvised skirmish line began methodically sweeping Central Field and clearing tents of Japanese, often by flamethrower. Fighting to the death, the Japanese survivors fled into open trenches, which USAAF personnel began tossing grenades into with great relish. By 0700hrs the harrowing surprise attack had finally been crushed, with 262 Japanese killed and 18 taken prisoner. The Americans had lost 53 dead and 119 wounded; the USAAF alone had suffered 44 dead and nearly 100 wounded, with the 21st Fighter Group losing 11 P-51 pilots as casualties. Hours later, US authorities declared Iwo Jima officially secure and the miserable isle was duly relinquished to occupation authorities.

Iwo Jima's build-up as an American airbase continued. By April 1, tankers could deliver gasoline directly to Iwo through a submarine pipeline, while four 1,000gal. tanks were established ashore. By mid-April, Iwo would teem with 31,000 US military personnel, while the USAAF's 306th Fighter Group (111 P-47N Thunderbolts) would begin arriving on May 11. Meanwhile, the Japanese continued occasional night bombing raids against Iwo, with the last attempt on August 4.

Postwar records indicate the Japanese lost 732 total planes between February 1 and March 1, although relatively few were lost over Iwo Jima. Of 337 Japanese aircraft lost in combat, 24 were kamikazes. Two Japanese submarines and four picket ships were sunk, and five picket ships damaged.

Total US Iwo Jima casualties reached a staggering 22,114 men, with 5,519 killed and missing. Most were marines, although 1,254 were naval battle casualties, including 628 killed and missing. Kamikazes had sunk escort carrier *Bismarck Sea*. Another 30 US ships had been damaged, 15 to shore batteries, three to kamikazes, one to bombs, and 11 to operational causes. US forces had lost 168 aircraft, including 51 operationally.

ICEBERG PRELIMINARIES, MARCH 1945

Okinawa and the Ryukyus

Some 740nm west-northwest of Iwo Jima is the Nansei Shoto or Ryukyus island chain, which Japan had formally annexed in 1879. The Ryukyus are a 650nm-long arc of 161 islands extending from Kyushu south-southwest to Formosa. The Ryukyus' long north–south arc separates the Philippine Sea in the east from the East China Sea to the west. The Ryukyus' largest island, Okinawa, lies 350nm south of Kyushu. At 66nm long and about 7nm wide, Okinawa comprises one-fourth of the Ryukyus' land area. Four-fifths of Okinawa's 435,000 civilians lived in the southern third of the island, consisting of hilly, jumbled subsistence farmland. Okinawa's capital and largest city was Naha, population 60,000. Slightly smaller was Shuri and its ancient Shuri Castle, a veritable ridgetop fortress. Okinawa's south hosted five major airfields: Yontan, Kadena, Machinato, Naha, and Yonabaru. Okinawa's more rugged northern two-thirds are mountainous and forested, reaching 1,634ft ASL at Mount Yonaha. Five miles off northwestern Okinawa is the island of Ie Shima, which hosted a sixth major airfield. Okinawa's subtropical climate is hot and humid, with drenching, weeks-long summer rains.

Defending Okinawa was Lieutenant-General Mitsuru Ushijima's IJA 32nd Army, totaling 77,000 regular troops, plus 20,000 conscripted Okinawans. IJA units included four 75mm and three 20mm antiaircraft battalions, plus 400 *Maru-re* suicide boats hidden in concealed coves. Rear Admiral Minoru Ota's 3,825 sailors and 6,000 civilian conscripts manned Okinawa's Naval Base Force. These included several land-based air groups, 15 coast defense companies (120mm and 140mm guns), four antiaircraft groups (157 x 120mm, 25mm, and 13.2mm AA guns), one mortar battery (18 x 81mm), the 33rd Midget Submarine Unit, and several *Shinyo* suicide boat squadrons. Ushijima's Okinawa battle mantra declared: *One plane for one warship. One boat for one ship. One man for ten of the enemy or one tank.*

Prelude to Iceberg

Back on October 10, 1944, Mitscher's 17 fast carriers had launched heavy surprise airstrikes against Okinawa and Ryukyus airfields in preparation for MacArthur's Leyte landings. Mitscher hit Ryukyus airfields again on January 3–4 and January 22, 1945, this time to prepare for the subsequent Luzon invasion. By March 1945, the US Fifth Air Force was well established in the Philippines and throughout the month hammered Formosa airfields in preparation for *Iceberg*. To Spruance's chagrin, by late March, Fifth Air Force had shifted to Formosan industrial targets, despite US intelligence estimating Formosa still retained 375 operational aircraft.

On March 18, Mitscher's TF-58 attacked 45 Kyushu airfields and claimed 102 Japanese planes shot down and 275 destroyed or damaged on the ground. Ugaki's Fifth Air Fleet counterattacked, hitting carriers *Enterprise*, *Intrepid*, and *Yorktown*, causing minor damage that killed seven Americans and wounded 69. TF-58's CAP and antiaircraft fire claimed 33 Japanese attackers.

The following morning, March 19, 436 TF-58 planes struck Inland Sea naval targets and shore facilities. Mitscher's strike damaged the battleships *Yamato*, *Ise*, *Hyuga*, and *Haruna*, the carriers *Amagi*, *Katsuragi*, and *Ryuho*, and numerous lesser warships, but lost 38 American aircraft. In return, Ugaki's morning counterstrike heavily damaged the carriers *Wasp* and *Franklin*. *Wasp* suffered 101 dead and 269 wounded but remained in action. *Franklin* was minutes from launching a major strike, and consequent secondary detonations immediately turned *Franklin* into a raging inferno. A hellish nine-hour battle ultimately saved the carrier. Covered by TF-58 fighters, cruiser *Pittsburgh* towed *Franklin* out of immediate danger. Total *Franklin* casualties were 798 killed and 487 wounded; she never returned to service. TF-58 then withdrew, having claimed 97 Japanese planes shot down and 225 more destroyed or damaged on the ground for March 19.

A stricken carrier *Franklin* blazes off Shikoku, March 19, 1945. Her visible list to starboard is entirely due to firefighting water. *Franklin* was the worst-damaged US ship to survive the war. The photograph was taken from light cruiser *Santa Fe*, which came alongside to assist. (Corbis via Getty Images)

The following afternoon, March 20, TF-58 was attacked by 15 enemy aircraft. Fourteen were destroyed, but the last attacker overshot carrier *Hancock* and crashed destroyer *Halsey Powell* (DD-686), killing 12 and wounding 29. During the action, friendly antiaircraft fire started fires aboard *Enterprise*, destroying eight planes and disabling air operations. An additional eight torpedo bombers unsuccessfully attacked TF-58 at 2300hrs, although TF-58 antiaircraft fire splashed three snoopers overnight.

At 1400hrs, March 21, TF-58 radar detected a large formation 100nm to the northwest. TF-58 scrambled 150 fighters. About 50nm from the carriers they intercepted 32 G4M Betties and 16 escorting fighters of the 721st Kokutai. All 48 IJN planes were destroyed for the loss of two US fighters. Post-action photographic analysis revealed the Betties to have been carrying *Ohka* rockets, the type's first operational appearance.

Between March 17 and March 21, Ugaki had thrown 241 planes against TF-58 and lost 161. Despite inflicting significant damage, Fifth Air Fleet had not materially affected Spruance's *Iceberg* operations. In turn, Fifth Air Fleet needed several weeks to recover, by which time US forces would be firmly ashore at Okinawa. Ugaki's March 17–21 air attacks proved an operational and strategic failure.

On March 22 Mitscher assigned damaged carriers *Franklin*, *Wasp*, and *Enterprise* to a reorganized TG-58.2, which was then dispatched to Ulithi for repairs. Except for April 8–17, when TG-58.2 was briefly reestablished, TF-58 strength would remain at three Task Groups throughout *Iceberg*'s duration.

TF-58 kicked off *Iceberg* at 0028hrs, March 23, when destroyer *Haggard* (DD-555) rammed and sank Japanese submarine *RO-41*. Hours later, TF-58 commenced daily strikes on Okinawa. During *Iceberg*, weather would prevent TF-58 operations on just five days. Refueling and replenishment operations were typically every fourth day. Between March 23 and April 28, such operations would allow an average of two Task Groups to provide daily support off Okinawa. After April 28, at least one Task Group would

A TF-58 fighter's color gun camera captures a G4M Betty bomber moments before shooting it down, March 21, 1945. US pilots noticed the Betties were flying slower than usual and looked strange. Post-action photographic analysis showed the Betties were carrying *Ohka* rockets, their very first operational appearance. (US Navy)

LSM(R)-196, *LSM(R)-190*, and *LSM(R)-199* unleash rocket volleys at Japanese positions on Kerama Retto, March 26, 1945. Each LSM(R)-188-class ship could saturate a target with 480 unguided 5in. rockets in 30 seconds, but then required several hours to reload. (US Navy)

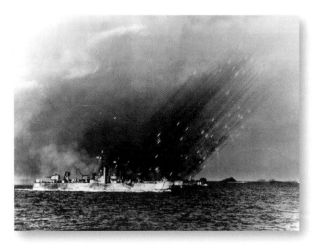

always directly support *Iceberg*, with two Task Groups directly supporting *Iceberg* two days out of four.

To prepare for *Iceberg*'s imminent minesweeping operations, TF-58 launched "extensive bombing attacks of all known installations including coastal batteries." TF-58 additionally obtained complete photoreconnaissance coverage, which it delivered to Turner's TF-51 just prior to landings. On March 24, TF-58 airpower covered TG-52.2 minesweepers arriving off Okinawa and Kerama Retto. Almost as an aside, reconnaissance discovered an eight-ship Japanese convoy 150nm northwest of Okinawa. A 112-plane TG-58.1 strike duly annihilated it. US losses were three Avengers.

Kerama Retto and Keise Shima, March 25–31

Twenty miles off southwestern Okinawa is the Kerama Retto, a cluster of ten small, hilly islands partially sheltering a potential anchorage. Against initial USN opposition, Turner had insisted on preemptively seizing Kerama Retto for use as an advanced staging base and as a temporary shelter for damaged ships. Additionally, the islets of Keise Shima, 11nm southwest of the Hagushi landing beaches, would be seized on L-1 to emplace heavy artillery. The US 77th Division was assigned both tasks. Landing and supporting it was the Western Island Attack Force (TG-51.1), commanded by Rear Admiral Ingolf Kiland aboard amphibious command ship *Mount McKinley* (AGC-7).

US carrier aircraft began striking Kerama Retto on March 25, while Kiland's TG-51.1 arrived off Kerama Retto the following morning. Supported by naval gunfire, including battleship *Arkansas* and cruisers *San Francisco* and *Minneapolis*, BLTs of the US 77th Division came ashore at several islands in the steep and rugged archipelago and began methodically clearing Japanese resistance. However, off Kerama Retto the following day, destroyer *O'Brien* (DD-725) suffered 50 dead and 76 wounded when a bomb-laden D3A Val crashed amidships and detonated a magazine. Nevertheless, by March 28, organized resistance on Kerama Retto had ceased, having cost 77th Division 31 killed and 81 wounded. Additionally, over 350 suicide boats were discovered in Kerama Retto caves and destroyed.

Shortly nicknamed the "demolition yard," Kerama's anchorage would prove invaluable for saving battle-damaged US warships. Kerama's roadstead would also receive Victory-class ammunition ships from the US West Coast. Supported by bomb- and shell-laden LSTs, the Victory ships would replenish TF-51 at Kerama or off Hagushi in a bold new forward ammunition replenishment system. Additionally, West Coast-based commercial tankers would supply petroleum to Ulithi, where 40 fleet oilers would then shuttle it to

Operation *Iceberg*, March 25–June 21, 1945

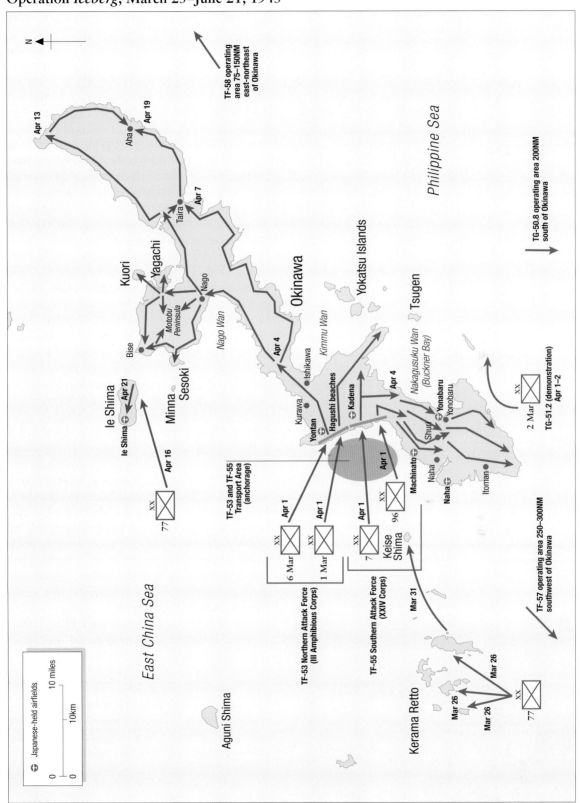

the Ryukyus for *Iceberg* operations. During mid-April US tankers would supply Fifth Fleet with 167,000 barrels of fuel oil and 385,000gals of avgas per day.

By March 29, FAW-1, totaling 30 PBM Mariner seaplanes, had arrived at Kerama Retto and begun patrol operations. Two days later, at the islets of Keise Shima, Seabees helped TG-51.1's LSTs and LSMs land and emplace 24 155mm guns of the 420th Field Artillery. Within hours these batteries would provide heavy L-Day fire support for the main landings.

Rawlings' TF-57 strikes the Sakishima Gunto, March 26–31

To initiate the British, Spruance had assigned Rawlings' semi-independent TF-57 the supporting role of suppressing airfields in the Sakishima Gunto, a Ryukyus archipelago 200nm southwest of Okinawa and 150nm east of Formosa. TF-57 arrived 100nm south of the eastern Sakishimas at dawn on March 26 and launched a 48-strong fighter sweep against airfields at Miyako, followed by two escorted Avenger strikes and a Hellcat fighter–bomber raid. However, throughout March 26, TF-57 was dogged by patrolling USN PB4Y-1 bombers that drifted into TF-57 airspace without activating their IFF (Identification Friend or Foe) equipment. That evening TF-57 withdrew southeast for the night, having lost nine planes and three airmen. By dawn, March 27, TF-57 had returned to repeat the Miyako airfield suppression as well as attack coastal shipping. A subsequent typhoon report inspired Rawlings to retire south to refuel. TF-57 resumed Sakishima strikes on March 31, again preceded by fighter sweeps, before retiring overnight to prepare for L-Day.

US sailors investigate the wreck of destroyer USS *Halligan* (DD-584) on March 28, 1945. Two days earlier *Halligan* had unwittingly hit a Japanese mine and exploded. After being abandoned, *Halligan* drifted 12 miles overnight before coming to rest here at Tokashiki Island just off Okinawa. (NHHC 80-G-324187)

Okinawa: Countdown to L-Day, March 25–31

Mitscher's TF-58 cruised to the north and east of Okinawa. On March 25, TF-58 aircraft splashed three Japanese planes over Okinawa and strafed another 45 at Okinawa airfields. Additionally, as part of *Iceberg*'s diversionary feint away from the true landing zone, Mitscher detached Rear Admiral L.E. Denfeld's fast battleships *New Jersey*, *Wisconsin*, *Missouri*, and five destroyers to bombard southeastern Okinawa. Fast battleships *Massachusetts* and *Indiana*, plus six destroyers, bombarded a second diversionary beach. Simultaneously, Blandy's TF-52 deployed to the west and north of Okinawa, to prepare Tenth Army landing zones and block potential IJN surface attacks or relief attempts.

Durgin's Escort Carrier Groups (TG-52.1) comprised 18 escort carriers and 538 aircraft. A total of 26 escort carriers would eventually participate in *Iceberg*, plus four more in a supply role. They had begun striking Okinawa and Kerama Retto on March 25. Additionally, TG-52.1 would temporarily assume Sakishima strikes during TF-57's March 29–30 refueling. Durgin's escort carriers would ultimately mount over 3,000 sorties against Okinawa targets by L-Day.

Nine kamikazes attacked US ships off Okinawa on March 26. One of them, a

D4Y Val, crashed radar picket destroyer *Kimberley* (DD-521), killing four and wounding 57. Another Val caromed off destroyer-transport *Gilmer* (APD-11), killing one and wounding three. That same day the Mine Flotilla commenced sweeping operations. Nonetheless, destroyer *Halligan* (DD-584) stumbled into an unswept area 12nm west of Naha, struck a mine, and sank. *Halligan* suffered 153 killed and 39 wounded. Two days later minesweeper *Skylark* (AM-63) would strike two mines and sink, suffering five dead and 25 wounded.

The Task Group 58.1 flagship, Essex-class fast carrier *Hornet*, cruises off Okinawa on March 27, 1945. *Hornet* wears camouflage Measure 33, Design 3a, which was intended to confuse submarine ranging. The Essexes were the backbone of Task Force 58, carrying about 100 planes each. (NHHC 80-G-K-14466)

At dawn, March 27, seven kamikazes suddenly attacked TF-54. Two were splashed, but one crashed battleship *Nevada*, killing 11 men and wounding 49. A fourth kamikaze holed light cruiser *Biloxi* in the waterline. *Biloxi*, shipping the kamikaze's undetonated 1,100lb bomb in a flooded compartment, retired to Kerama Retto without loss. Destroyer-minesweeper *Dorsey* (DMS-1) was glanced by a kamikaze, killing three and wounding two. Meanwhile, a single B6N Jill was shot down attacking TF-58. Its torpedo passed completely through destroyer *Murray* (DD-576), slightly damaging her. Overnight March 28/29 air raids wrecked *LSM(R)-188*, killing 15 and injuring 32, and damaged attack cargo ship *Wyandot* (AKA-92), wounding one.

That same night LCIs and *LSM(R)-189* destroyed six Japanese suicide boats. Throughout *Iceberg*, TF-51 would counter marauding Japanese boats by assigning LCI(G) gunboat flotillas to specific patrol zones ringing Okinawa. Backed by a cruiser or destroyer further offshore, these so-called "Flycatcher" patrols would destroy 71 suicide boats by May 17. The "Flycatchers" would also intercept attempted Japanese counterlandings behind US lines.

On March 29, TG-58.3's five fast carriers launched 172 sorties against Kyushu air facilities, but deteriorating weather prematurely ended strikes that afternoon. Meanwhile, B-29s of Major-General Curtis LeMay's Marianas-based XXI Bomber Command, shanghaied into supporting *Iceberg*, had already struck Kyushu airfields two days earlier. They would hit Kyushu again on March 31, before dropping 5,656 tons of bombs on Kyushu airbases through April. Despite their dubious effectiveness against airfields, LeMay's B-29s would continue intermittent Kyushu raids until released from *Iceberg* support on May 11.

By late March 29 the "largest assault sweep operation ever executed" had cleared the Hagushi beach approaches in 75 sweeps, with US minesweepers having cleared 3,000 square miles of littoral. The following morning, TF-54's ten battleships and 11 cruisers closed to shell Okinawa defenses and smash coastal seawalls. They would deliver over 25,000 tons of ordnance by May 16. Meanwhile, UDT frogmen began scouting and clearing the Hagushi landing beaches.

Durgin's escort carriers launched airstrikes against recently discovered submarine pens in Okinawan coves. On April 5, a single midget submarine would fire a torpedo at transport *Catron* (APA-71), which missed. Indeed, Japanese submarine reaction to *Iceberg* proved lackluster. Destroyers

Morrison (DD-560) and *Stockton* (DD-646) would sink *I-8* on March 31, while *RO-49* would succumb to *Hudson* (DD-475) on April 5, followed by *RO-56* to *Monssen* (DD-798) and *Mertz* (DD-691) on April 9.

At 0707hrs, March 31, a Ki-43 Oscar crashed Spruance's flagship *Indianapolis*, killing nine and critically damaging a shaft. *Indianapolis* departed stateside for repairs, leaving Spruance to transfer flag to battleship *New Mexico* on April 5. About 44 Japanese aircraft had attacked TF-51 between March 26 and March 31, with 24 estimated destroyed or crashed. Another 20–30 Japanese planes had heckled TF-51 overnight, with 14 destroyed.

The morning of March 31 saw US gunships cover the frogmen's last Hagushi demolition operations, then resume hammering Japanese defensive positions. In the final week to L-Day, Fifth Fleet had hurled 19,850 battleship and cruiser main battery rounds into Okinawa positions, plus 50,000 5in. shells. Additionally, Mitscher's TG-58.3 and TG-58.4 flew CAPs and launched sweeps and strikes against Okinawa, concentrating on targets unreachable by naval gunfire. However, the pounding was largely wasted, as Ushijima's men had withdrawn inland. American firepower nevertheless razed Naha and Shuri, probably killing thousands of civilians. Indeed, the invasion's enormous weight of air, naval, and ground-based bombardment would inspire Okinawans to dub the battle *Tetsu no ame*: "Rain of steel."

L-DAY AT OKINAWA, APRIL 1

For *Iceberg*, Turner's Joint Expeditionary Force (TF-51) had been reinforced to 1,213 ships staging from Espíritu Santu, Guadalcanal, the Russells, Saipan, Guam, Eniwetok, New Caledonia, Leyte, Oahu, and the US West Coast. *Iceberg* would require eight transport squadrons to land four divisions simultaneously. Each transport squadron comprised 15 attack transports, six attack cargo ships, 25 LSTs, ten LSMs, and one LSD. A combined 179 attack transports and 187 LSTs would carry the 172,000 assault troops and 115,000 service support troops that would come ashore in early April. When Turner's TF-51 was combined with Mitscher's TF-58, the Royal Navy's TF-57, and Spruance's supporting forward logistic groups, *Iceberg*'s Fifth Fleet exceeded 1,600 ships, eclipsing June 1944's *Overlord/Neptune* flotilla as the largest armada in history. With over 1,400 American ships, Fifth Fleet was certainly the largest national fleet ever assembled.

During *Iceberg*, Mitscher's Fast Carrier Task Force, TF-58, would deploy roughly 70nm east of Okinawa, while Turner's Joint Expeditionary Force, TF-51, would closely surround Okinawa's shoreline in six concentric defensive and tactical support zones, with Turner's main transport anchorage a few miles off western Okinawa's Hagushi beaches. Supporting both task forces was Beary's Logistic Support Group,

New Mexico-class battleship *Idaho* bombards Okinawa with her 14in./50 main guns, April 1, 1945. She was photographed from battleship *West Virginia*. The near-horizontal angle of *Idaho's* guns betrays her point-blank range. *Idaho* and her sisters *New Mexico* and *Mississippi* had patrolled the Atlantic in 1941 but were transferred to the Pacific after Pearl Harbor. (NHHC 80-G-K-3829)

TG-50.8, which cruised 200nm south of Okinawa. The Royal Navy's fast carriers, TF-57, would remain deployed halfway between Okinawa and Formosa.

The recent loss of *Wasp*, *Franklin*, and *Enterprise* had reduced Fifth Fleet's L-Day carrier strength to 1,727 aircraft. TF-58's fast carriers, TG-52.1's escort carriers, and eventually the ground-based TAF would maintain daily CAPs over Fifth Fleet; these would vary between 48 and 120 fighters. Backstopping the CAPs were naval antiaircraft batteries. Between April 1 and June 30, 1945, US ships off Okinawa would fire on 1,898 Japanese planes, including 785 confirmed kamikazes. April 1945 would be the USN's

Laden with assault troops, LVTs churn towards an L-Day touchdown at Okinawa's Hagushi beaches, April 1, 1945. Behind them, battleship *Tennessee* provides a thundering bombardment. LVTs had first tentatively served in an assault capacity at Tarawa, where US authorities quickly recognized them as indispensable. (Public Domain)

most active month of the war in terms of antiaircraft engagements, with activity in May falling to 50 percent of April, and then to just 10 percent in June. Turner's TF-51 alone would count 560 raids by 2,228 Japanese planes between April 1 and May 17.

On L-Day, Deyo's TF-54 of ten slow battleships, nine cruisers, 23 destroyers, and 177 LCI(G) gunboats began bombarding Okinawa's western beaches, ultimately lobbing 3,800 tons of shells and rockets ashore in "the heaviest concentration of naval gunfire ever delivered in support of [an amphibious invasion]." Combined with TF-58, Spruance's Fifth Fleet would bombard Okinawa with 44,825 shells of 5in. or larger on April 1, ultimately expending 600,018 such shells by *Iceberg*'s conclusion.

At 0406hrs Turner ordered, "Land the landing force!" Total Okinawa assault personnel came to 182,112 troops: 98,567 US Army, 81,165 USMC, and 2,380 USN. They were accompanied by 286,635 tons of supplies. Each assault regiment streamed ashore in eight landing waves, deploying two BLTs abreast. The first waves comprised 28 LVT(A)(4) amtanks mounting 75mm howitzers. The second totaled 16 LVT(4)s carrying assault troops. Each of the subsequent third, fourth, fifth, and sixth waves numbered 12 LVT(4)s carrying assault troops and crew-served weapons. The following seventh waves consisted of LSMs or LCMs transporting amphibious M4 Sherman tanks, while LVT(4)s of the eighth and final waves landed support troops.

At 0830hrs Buckner's four assault divisions landed abreast on an eight-mile frontage at Hagushi beaches on the western side of Okinawa; the landings were the largest of the Pacific War. The Northern Attack Force (TF-53) landed the III Amphibious Corps' 6th and 1st Marine Divisions on the left (north), while the Southern Attack Force (TF-55) landed the XXIV US Corps' 7th and 96th Divisions on the right (south). Resistance was scant; within an hour 16,000 Americans were ashore. By 1116hrs, IIIAC had already captured Yontan airfield. Less than 90 minutes later XXIV Corps had occupied Kadena airfield. The virtually bloodless occupation of Yontan and Kadena, days ahead of schedule, proved a critical and unexpected victory.

Off Okinawa's eastern coast, Rear Admiral Jerauld Wright's Demonstration Group (TG-51.2) loaded 2nd Marine Division personnel into landing craft. Streaming for shore, the marines made landing feints against southeastern Okinawa's Minatogawa beaches, before intentionally aborting the charade landings at exactly 0830hrs—western Okinawa's actual touchdown. Unfortunately, Formosa-based 17th Sentai kamikazes had already slammed into transport *Hinsdale* (APA-120) and *LST-844*, killing 40 and wounding 60. Japanese defenders subsequently reported "enemy landing on east coast completely foiled with heavy losses to enemy." Wright's TG-51.2 would demonstrate again on April 2, to no great effect.

Nevertheless, at Hagushi over 60,000 US troops and marines were ashore by nightfall. Tenth Army had established a solid beachhead eight miles across and two miles deep. Battleships *West Virginia*, *Idaho*, *Nevada*, seven cruisers, and ten destroyers remained on station for overnight fire support calls, with harassment fire and battlefield illumination (starshells) major missions. The following day, XXIV Corps would reach Okinawa's east coast, severing Okinawa's north from south. Rugged, desolate northern Okinawa, lightly defended, saw relatively less fighting throughout the battle. In contrast, Tenth Army quickly encountered heavily fortified Japanese positions on its main drive into the populated, more strategic south, transforming the Okinawa ground campaign into a long, grueling battle of frontal attrition.

L-Day had found a disorganized Combined Fleet unprepared to launch mass kamikaze attacks, despite the Kerama Retto landings having triggered *Ten-Go* back on March 26. Nevertheless, 38 kamikazes had sortied from Kyushu and Formosa on April 1 to counter the US landings. At 0550hrs, seven Formosa-based Ki-61 Tonies had crashed destroyer-minelayer *Adams* (DM-27) and *LST-724*. Japanese conventional attacks would additionally damage destroyer *Prichett* (DD-561), minesweeper *Skirmish* (AM-303), and attack transport *Elmore* (APA-42). At 1903hrs, a kamikaze crashed battleship *West Virginia*, killing four. Seven minutes later two Japanese planes dove towards attack transport *Alpine* (APA-92). *Alpine* shot down one, but the second, only damaged, slammed blazing into *Alpine*'s port side, causing explosions and fires that killed 16 and wounded 27.

At 0043hrs, April 2, attack cargo ship *Achernar* (AKA-53) was hit almost simultaneously by a kamikaze and a separate bomb. She suffered five dead and 41 wounded and retired for repairs. Later at dusk, Second Lieutenant Okiteru Takeda's eight Ki-25 Nicks of the 114th Hikotai crashed transports *Goodhue* (APA-107) and *Telfair* (APA-210), inflicting a combined 25 killed and 135 wounded. A PY1 Frances bomber additionally slammed into the bridge of attack transport *Henrico* (APA-45), killing 49 and wounding 125. *Henrico* withdrew to Kerama Retto. Meanwhile, destroyer-transport *Dickerson* (APD-21) landed troops to capture Keise Shima off Okinawa, but that night was struck by two kamikazes, killing 54 and wounding 23. *Dickerson* was subsequently scuttled.

On April 3, some 119 Japanese aircraft sortied against Fifth Fleet. These comprised 20 conventional Judy bombers plus 24 kamikazes from IJN Fifth Air Fleet, escorted by 32 Zero and eight "George" Shiden-Kai fighters (84 IJN aircraft). IJA Sixth Air Army dispatched 35 attackers. Destroyer *Prichett* (DD-551) was

A blasted Zero goes down in flames while attacking escort carrier *Wake Island* (CVE-95) off Okinawa, April 3, 1945. This image is just one from a dramatic series of the incident, taken from nearby escort carrier *Tulagi* (CVE-72). (NHHC 80-G-339261)

struck in the fantail by a 500lb bomb, while at Kerama Retto, a kamikaze struck *LST-599* and the piggy-backed *LCT-876*, wounding 23. Nearby destroyer-escort *Foreman* (DE-633) was struck by a bomb, killing two and wounding three. *Foreman* withdrew to Ulithi. Southeast of Okinawa, escort carrier *Wake Island* (CVE-65) suffered damage from an unexpectedly huge wave, which was followed minutes later by a crashing kamikaze. *Wake Island* retired without loss to Guam. The following day, a kamikaze damaged destroyer *Wilson* (DD-408) off Kerama Retto. Later that night, a *Shinyo* suicide boat attacked and sank gunboat *LCI(G)-82* east of Okinawa, killing eight. Then on April 5, an Okinawa shore battery hit battleship *Nevada*, killing two.

TBM-3 Avengers raid Japanese targets during *Iceberg*, April 4, 1945. As late as March 29, some 20–30 Japanese planes were suddenly discovered at Yontan and shot up by FM-2 Wildcats from *Makin Island*. Another seven Japanese planes were strafed at nearby Kadena. (NHHC 80-G-319244)

THE GREAT ONSLAUGHT: *KIKISUI* NO. 1, APRIL 6–7

Japanese April 4–5 air action had been quiet, but thanks to signals intelligence, Spruance knew this was the calm before the storm. Early on April 6, Japanese aerial reconnaissance located two US carrier groups off Okinawa. At 1015hrs Ugaki's first kamikazes began launching from Kyushu airfields. Within hours, hundreds of Japanese planes were airborne. From Formosa the independent 8th Air Division and First Air Fleet contributed additional attacks. In this first and greatest *Kikisui*, 699 Japanese planes attacked over April 6–7, including 355 kamikazes (230 IJAAF and 125 IJNAF). The official USAAF history accordingly called *Kikisui* No. 1 "one of the most furious air counterattacks of the Pacific War."

Japanese aerial attacks, April 6
US carriers unleashed a combined 19 USN and four USMC squadrons to blunt the onslaught. Swirling, running dogfights developed around noon and lasted through sunset. April 6, 1945 may have started slow, but by evening it had developed into one of the greatest aerial confrontations of all time. American CAPs overwhelmingly massacred the poorly trained Japanese attackers; Mitscher's TF-58 fighters claimed 249 Japanese planes for just two lost—a staggering 125-to-1 kill ratio. Yet the kamikaze pilots' grim determination was chillingly apparent. According to VF-82's action report: "Of all the enemy planes encountered, *not one returned fire*, all remained on course, boring in toward the surface vessels. The only evasive action offered was jinking, and the majority of the aircraft were obsolete models as can be seen by the list [of] destroyed. Primary danger to our pilots was collision or getting in the path of a friendly plane's fire."

Essex's VF-83 (36 Hellcats) and VBF-83 (36 Corsairs) combined for 69 kills, while *Belleau Wood*'s 24 VF-30 Hellcats shot down 47. *Belleau Wood*'s skipper, Captain Red Tomlinson, duly signaled TG-58.1's Rear Admiral J.J. Jocko Clark: "Does this exceed the bag limit?" Clark responded, "Negative.

KIKISUI NO. 1, APRIL 6–7, 1945

Shown here are the major strikes against Allied naval assets off Okinawa and Kerama Retto.

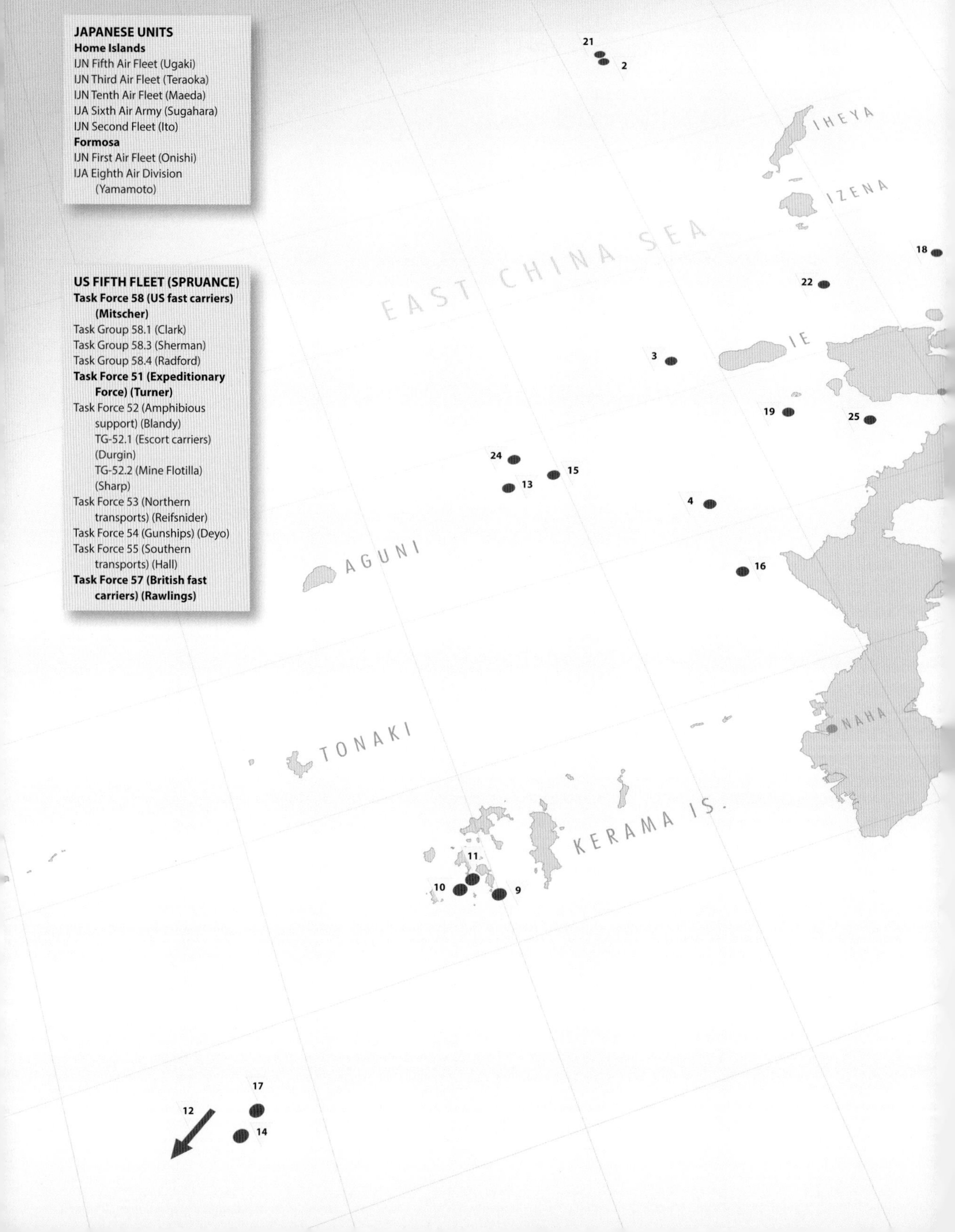

JAPANESE UNITS
Home Islands
IJN Fifth Air Fleet (Ugaki)
IJN Third Air Fleet (Teraoka)
IJN Tenth Air Fleet (Maeda)
IJA Sixth Air Army (Sugahara)
IJN Second Fleet (Ito)
Formosa
IJN First Air Fleet (Onishi)
IJA Eighth Air Division (Yamamoto)
US FIFTH FLEET (SPRUANCE)
Task Force 58 (US fast carriers) (Mitscher)
Task Group 58.1 (Clark)
Task Group 58.3 (Sherman)
Task Group 58.4 (Radford)
Task Force 51 (Expeditionary Force) (Turner)
Task Force 52 (Amphibious support) (Blandy)
TG-52.1 (Escort carriers) (Durgin)
TG-52.2 (Mine Flotilla) (Sharp)
Task Force 53 (Northern transports) (Reifsnider)
Task Force 54 (Gunships) (Deyo)
Task Force 55 (Southern transports) (Hall)
Task Force 57 (British fast carriers) (Rawlings)
EAST CHINA SEA
IHEYA
IZENA
IE
AGUNI
TONAKI
NAHA
KERAMA IS.
21
2
18
22
3
19
25
24
15
13
4
16
11
10
9
17
12
14

YORON

PHILIPPINE SEA

OKINAWA

MIYAGI

● 7

● 6   ● 20

● 8

EVENTS

April 6

1. East of Okinawa, TF-58 destroyer *Haynesworth* (DD-700) is the day's first ship struck by a kamikaze when she is crashed by a Judy at 1226hrs. Seven Americans are killed. Near-misses from kamikazes and bombs also damage nearby light carrier *San Jacinto* and destroyers *Harrison* (DD-573) and *Taussig* (DD-746).

2. At 1500hrs, about 50 Japanese planes appear over RPS-1 and begin attacking destroyer *Bush* (DD-529). *Bush* shoots down two but is crashed at 1510hrs. Destroyer *Colhoun* (DD-801) leaves her RPS-2 station to assist *Bush*, reaching *Bush* at 1635hrs. After *Colhoun* arrives, *Bush* and *Colhoun* combine to shoot down eight attackers, but *Colhoun* takes four kamikaze hits and *Bush* is hit by five total kamikazes. *Bush* sinks at 1830hrs, suffering 94 dead. *Colhoun* has lost 35 killed and is scuttled that night.

3. An A6M3 Hamp crashes destroyer *Hyman* (DD-732) at 1627hrs, killing ten. *Hyman* shoots down three attackers.

4. Destroyer *Howorth* (DD-592), headed to assist *Hyman*, is attacked by eight Zeros at 1700hrs. *Howorth* splashes five but suffers one kamikaze hit, killing nine.

5. Three kamikazes hit destroyer-minesweeper *Rodman* (DMS-21) that afternoon. Assisting destroyer-minesweeper *Emmons* (DMS-22) shoots down six but at 1732hrs is suddenly hit by five kamikazes over two minutes, killing 64. *Emmons* is later scuttled.

6. At 1612hrs, a Val crashes destroyer-escort *Witter* (DE-636), killing six.

7. Almost simultaneously, two kamikazes crash destroyer *Mullany* (DD-528), killing 30.

8. Later, at 1815hrs, a kamikaze hits destroyer *Morris* (DD-417), killing 13 and wounding 45.

9. Numerous kamikazes penetrate Kerama Retto, where at 1627hrs a damaged Zero crashes *LST-447*. She sinks the next day, having lost five men.

10. Simultaneously, another kamikaze hits ammunition freighter *Logan Victory*, killing 16. *Logan Victory* is eventually scuttled.

11. Having shot down one plane, nearby *Hobbs Victory* stands out from Kerama, but at 1845hrs is also crashed by a kamikaze. Resulting fires force *Hobbs Victory*'s abandonment. The following morning *Hobbs Victory* explodes and sinks, having lost 15 dead.

12. Southwest of this map, off the Sakishima Gunto, a diving kamikaze grazes British carrier *Illustrious* at 1700hrs. Its bomb detonates underwater.

13. Screening minesweepers, beginning at 1800hrs destroyer *Newcomb* (DD-586) is hit by three kamikazes and destroyer *Leutze* (DD-481) by a fourth kamikaze while assisting *Newcomb*.

14. Kamikaze attack damages minesweeper *Facility* (AM-233).

15. Two kamikazes crash minesweeper *Defense* (AM-317).

16. Kamikaze attack damages minesweepers *Devastator* (AM-318) and *Recruit* (AM-285).

17. Horizontal bomber damages destroyer-minesweeper *Harding* (DMS-28).

18. Kamikaze attack damages destroyer-escort *Fieberling* (DE-640) and minesweeper *Ransom* (AM-283).

19. Kamikaze attack damages motor minesweeper *YMS-311*.

20. Kamikaze attack damages motor minesweeper *YMS-321*.

April 7

21. At 0850hrs destroyer *Bennett* (DD-473), at RPS-1, is crashed by a Val, killing three and wounding 18.

22. At 0917hrs a kamikaze crashes destroyer-escort *Wesson* (DE-184), killing seven.

23. At 1212hrs a Japanese plane first bombs, then crashes TF-58 fast carrier *Hancock*, causing fires and moderate damage that is largely under control by 1300hrs. *Hancock* suffers 72 dead and 82 wounded.

24. At dusk, a kamikaze crashes battleship *Maryland* on her No. 3 16in. turret, inflicting 53 casualties.

25. Kamikaze attack damages motor minesweeper *YMS-81*.

A US enlisted man updates the vertical plotting board in a darkened Essex-class Combat Information Center (CIC). Radar returns (and information from visual lookouts) were channeled to the ship's specialized CIC, where trained ratings tracked radar contacts on specialized plotting boards. From here a highly trained Fighter Director officer directed fighter interceptions over voice radio. (Photo by Edward Steichen/George Eastman Museum/Getty Images)

There is no limit. This is open season. Well done."

The US carrier fighters' 275 kills was the war's fourth-highest one-day total. Thirteen US pilots achieved ace status (scored their fifth kill) on April 6, with four becoming "ace-in-a-day." Ten pilots claimed four kills, while another 17 shot down three each. Combined with antiaircraft fire, the Americans destroyed 355 Japanese planes.

But even overwhelming aerial victories proved insufficient against mass kamikaze attacks. Turner's TF-51 reported: "Commencing about 1500hrs, violent air attacks were pressed home against our ships. Patrol and picket stations were the main targets." Turner estimated that 182 Japanese aircraft in 22 groups attacked TF-51 that afternoon. American fighters and antiaircraft fire whittled that in half, but 24 kamikazes successfully crashed Fifth Fleet ships. April 6's high seas and cold temperatures would further endanger American survivors.

At 1226hrs, TF-58 destroyer *Haynesworth* (DD-700), east of Okinawa, was the first ship struck by kamikaze when a Judy crashed her, killing seven and injuring 25. Kamikaze and bomb near-misses would additionally damage light carrier *San Jacinto* (CVL-30) and destroyers *Harrison* (DD-573) and *Taussig* (DD-746).

Assigned to radar picket stations RPS-1, RPS-2, and RPS-3 respectively were destroyers *Bush* (DD-529), *Colhoun* (DD-801), and *Cassin Young* (DD-793). By dawn, *Colhoun* had already been bombed and missed by 11 separate attackers. Then around 1500hrs came 40–50 stacked, orbiting Japanese planes from the main *Kikisui*, which began attacking *Bush*. Another 12 Japanese planes attacked *Cassin Young* to the east. *Bush* shot down two before a kamikaze crashed her at 1510hrs.

Making 35kts, *Colhoun* reached the smoking, sinking *Bush* at 1635hrs. At 1700hrs, *Colhoun* shot down three attackers, but a fourth slammed blazing into *Colhoun*. Two minutes later *Bush* and *Colhoun* each splashed two more kamikazes, but the third crashed *Colhoun*, its detonating bomb breaking *Colhoun*'s keel and ripping her open to the sea. At 1725hrs came *Colhoun*'s sixth (and *Bush*'s fourth) attack of the day. Now dead in the water, *Colhoun* destroyed one attacker, but the second struck *Colhoun*, and two more smashed into *Bush*. Although both destroyers were sinking, *Cassin Young* (DD-793) and a tug were hard en route. One last kamikaze suddenly appeared at 1800hrs and slammed into the dying *Colhoun*, despite multiple hits from antiaircraft fire. Thirty minutes later the shattered *Bush* jackknifed in the heavy seas and went under. *Bush* lost 94 killed out of 333, including DesDiv-98 skipper Commander J.S. Willis. That night *Cassin Young* would scuttle *Colhoun* with gunfire; *Colhoun* had suffered 35 men killed and 21 wounded.

Meanwhile, destroyer *Hyman* (DD-732) was steaming towards her assigned "Flycatcher" picket station when an A6M3 Hamp crashed directly into her torpedo tubes. The Hamp, its bomb, and multiple torpedo warheads detonated, causing a huge fireball that killed ten men and wounded 40. Heading to assist *Hyman*, destroyer *Howorth* (DD-592) was immediately attacked by eight Zeros. *Howorth* shot down five but the sixth smashed into her, spraying burning gasoline over her bridge and killing nine. Both *Hyman* and *Howorth* detached to Kerama Retto for repairs.

The Mine Flotilla (TG-52.2) was particularly hard-hit. That afternoon, while covering minecraft sweeping the channel between Okinawa and Iheya Retto, destroyer-minesweeper *Rodman* (DMS-21) absorbed three kamikazes. Protectively circling *Rodman*, destroyer-minesweeper *Emmons* (DMS-22) shot down six attackers, while overhead USMC Corsairs claimed 20 more. But beginning at 1732hrs, *Emmons* was suddenly hit by five kamikazes and four near-misses in rapid succession, killing 64 Americans and wounding 71. *Emmons* would be scuttled the following day.

Screening minesweepers south of Ie Shima, destroyer *Leutze* (DD-481) fired on a Zero around 1800hrs, which suddenly swerved and crashed into destroyer *Newcomb* (DD-586) 4,000yds distant. *Leutze* shot down another kamikaze making a suicide run from 8,000yds, before closing *Newcomb* to assist. *Newcomb* then exploded from a second kamikaze hit. With *Leutze*'s heavy antiaircraft fire blocked by *Newcomb*'s superstructure, a third kamikaze slammed into the blazing *Newcomb*, now dead in the water and billowing smoke 1,000ft high. At 1815hrs another Zero appeared. At 1,000yds, a *Newcomb* 5in. shell exploded beneath the Zero, deflecting it away from *Newcomb*'s bridge to skim across *Newcomb*'s deck and then slam into *Leutze*'s waterline. The Zero's 550lb bomb exploded, ripping *Leutze*'s hull open and wrecking her steering. By 1830hrs *Leutze*'s fantail was awash. Radical damage control efforts lightened *Leutze* and likely saved her. Minesweeper *Defense* (AM-317), having already taken two kamikaze hits herself, began towing *Leutze* towards Kerama Retto. Upon reaching the anchorage, *Defense* cheekily signaled, "Sorry to be late, have scratched a kamikaze and taken two on board. Now have destroyer in tow." *Leutze* had suffered seven killed and 34 wounded. Joining her was the disabled *Newcomb*, towed to Kerama Retto with 40 dead and 24 wounded.

Photographed from seaplane tender *Chandeleur* (AV-10), US ships counter a dusk kamikaze attack against Kerama Retto, April 6, 1945. The bright flash is likely a kamikaze exploding. Kerama Retto raids that evening would ultimately sink two US freighters loaded with 14,000 tons of ammunition. (NHHC 80-G-311871)

US fast carrier *Hancock* burns after being hit by a kamikaze, April 7, 1945. *Hancock*'s gunners had shot the diving plane multiple times, but it and its 550lb bomb still crashed into *Hancock*. The resulting fires took an hour and a half to bring under control. (US Navy and Marine Corps Museum/ Naval Aviation Museum, 1983.046.010.135)

At 1612hrs a Val crashed destroyer-escort *Witter* (DE-636), killing six. Almost simultaneously, two kamikazes crashed destroyer *Mullany* (DD-528), on antisubmarine patrol. Abandoned and then reboarded, *Mullany* eventually made Kerama Retto under her own power, losing 30 dead. Destroyer *Morris* (DD-417) was hit by one kamikaze at 1815hrs, suffering 13 killed and 45 wounded.

Numerous kamikazes penetrated Kerama Retto, where a damaged Zero dove into *LST-447* at 1627hrs, its bomb detonating. The burning, abandoned LST ultimately sank, suffering five men missing and 17 wounded. Another kamikaze hit freighter *Logan Victory*, carrying 7,000 tons of ammunition. The fatally damaged *Logan Victory* lost 16 dead and 11 wounded. A few hours later, two kamikazes attacked *Hobbs Victory*, also carrying ammunition. *Hobbs Victory* splashed one but the second slammed into her, causing lethal fires that forced her abandonment. The following morning *Hobbs Victory* exploded and sank, having lost 15 killed and three wounded.

Ugaki erroneously reported two carriers, two battleships, three cruisers, eight destroyers, and five transports sunk. Kamikazes had in fact hit 20 ships and sunk six, although none larger than a destroyer. Conventional attacks had damaged several more. Allied casualties reached 370 men killed and another 475 wounded. However, April 6 proved the height of the kamikaze onslaught—never again could Japan mount such a large, coordinated single-day attack.

Japanese aerial attacks, April 7

Four new escort carriers had arrived off Okinawa on April 6. They carried TAF's first 222 fighters—192 Corsairs and 30 F6F-5N Hellcats of MAG-31 and MAG-33. By 1000hrs the following morning, TAF had established its headquarters ashore at Yontan, and the escort carriers had begun launching their charges to their new home. While en route, VMF-311 Corsairs scored TAF's first kill. By evening 90 F4U Corsairs and 15 F6F-5N Hellcats of VMF-224, VMF-311, VMF-441, and VMF-542(N) had transferred to Yontan.

Around noon, some 54 kamikazes escorted by 78 Zeros sortied towards TF-58, which was operating 70nm east of Okinawa. TF-58 fighters shot down 54 attackers, but at 1212hrs a D4Y Judy planted a bomb on fast

TF-57 during *Iceberg*, March 26–May 25, 1945

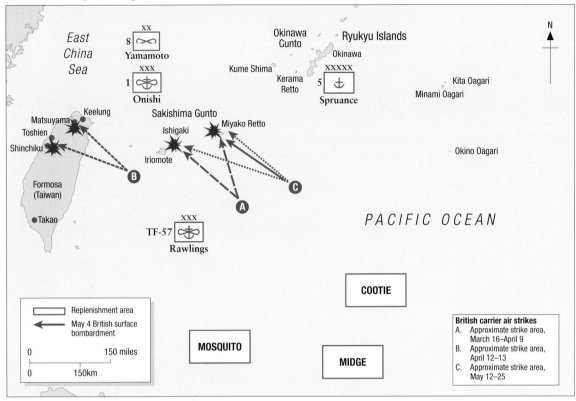

carrier *Hancock* before crashing across her deck, causing fires and explosions that killed 72 and wounded 82. *Hancock* shortly detached to Pearl Harbor. Across Fifth Fleet, kamikazes additionally damaged destroyer *Bennett* (DD-473), destroyer-escort *Wesson* (DE-184), and motor minesweeper *YMS-81*. At dusk, a bomb-laden kamikaze crashed battleship *Maryland*'s 16in turret, killing 16 and wounding 37. *Maryland* remained on station, but a week later permanently detached to Puget Sound.

Not all suicide attackers were eager to die. That afternoon Mitscher signaled that a kamikaze pilot had been picked up "from a fancy red life raft, wearing silk scarf with Nip inscription 'Kamikaze Special Attack Unit 3.' Says he flew from Kikai Jima. Graduated from Kisarazu late 1944 and is a flight instructor. Now matriculating in *Hornet*."

The combined April 6–7 *Kikisui* attacks would ultimately claim 485 Americans killed and 582 wounded. Nevertheless, severely depleted Japanese resources and personnel prevented Ugaki from mounting another mass *Kikisui* attack for five days. In the interim, daily small-scale kamikaze attacks would continue. This pattern of intermittent mass *Kikisui*, punctuated by small but persistent daily raids, would continue throughout the Okinawa battle.

Rawlings' TF-57 strikes the Sakishima Gunto, April 1–7

At dawn, on April 1, TF-57 struck Sakishima before immediately falling under Japanese attack. At 0725hrs a Zero strafed first *Indomitable* and then *King George V*; three minutes later a bomb-laden Zero crashed into the base of *Indefatigable*'s island, killing 14 and wounding 15. That

DEFENDING HMS *INDEFATIGABLE* OFF THE SAKISHIMA GUNTO, APRIL 1, 1945 (PP.52–53)

At 0645hrs, April 1, three bomb-laden Zeros of the 205th Kokutai sortied from the island of Ishigaki. They were led by Sub-Lieutenant Masatoshi Sakai. As per standard kamikaze doctrine, Sakai's three suicide planes were accompanied by a fourth Zero, intended for escort and observation. Sakai's target was the British fast carrier group, Task Force 57.

Sakai's flight was part of a larger Japanese attack that morning. British radar picket destroyers detected the approaching Japanese at 0645hrs. Range was 75nm. Although the British CAP shot down four Zeros, several got through, including one of Sakai's planes (**1**), which headed for carrier *Indefatigable* (**2**).

In hot pursuit was *Indefatigable*'s own Sub-Lieutenant Richard Reynolds, flying a Seafire III (**3**) from the 894 NAS. Flying through his own ships' antiaircraft fire, Reynolds hit the attacking Zero

several times as it plunged towards *Indefatigable*. This scene depicts Reynolds' Seafire chasing the diving kamikaze just moments before it impacted *Indefatigable*. Reynolds had to pull up to avoid slamming into *Indefatigable* himself.

The Japanese suicide was most likely aiming for *Indefatigable*'s funnel but missed, slamming into the base of *Indefatigable*'s island, which caused its 551lb bomb to detonate. The flight deck was buckled at the point of impact and *Indefatigable*'s island was blackened from the resulting fire, while additional damage was sustained in a sickbay and briefing room. Fourteen British sailors were killed, but repairs got *Indefatigable* back into action within eight hours. Although the pursuit depicted here had been in vain, minutes later Reynolds would successfully shoot down two Japanese attackers.

afternoon, a Zero clipped the portside flight deck of the maneuvering *Victorious*, causing the plane to cartwheel into the sea 80ft away. The Zero's 550lb bomb exploded dramatically but harmlessly, showering *Victorious* with tons of seawater, fuel, and debris. The combined Japanese attacks cost 15 British dead and 21 wounded. After a dawn fighter sweep the following day, TF-57 retired to replenish. Nimitz signaled congratulations to TF-57 for its "illustrious" performance, to which Rawlings responded that TF-57 would pursue the enemy "indomitably, indefatigably, and victoriously."

A diving D4Y Judy and its detonating 1,700lb bomb just misses British fast carrier *Illustrious*, April 6, 1945. A split-second earlier the Judy's wingtip had clipped *Illustrious'* island just 9ft from her captain. *Illustrious* suffered no casualties, but the underwater detonation crippled her propellor shaft. (ullstein bild via Getty Images)

High seas hampered TF-57's April 4–5 replenishing. As TG-58.1 had to cover the Sakishima Gunto while TF-57 refueled, Rawlings aborted early, even though battleships *Howe* and *King George V* remained half empty and the carriers only had avgas for two days' operations. TF-57 duly launched five strikes on April 6–7, losing ten planes, while a single kamikaze grazed *Illustrious*.

TEN-ICHI-GO: *YAMATO'S* DEATH RIDE, APRIL 6–7

Anticipating the US assault on Okinawa, on March 29, IJN and IJA officers had reviewed *Ten-Go* with Hirohito. The Emperor, himself a former IJN battleship officer, suddenly asked, "But what about the Navy? What are they doing to assist in defending Okinawa? Have we no more ships?"

Outraged at the perceived slight, the IJN's fiery, radical staff officer Captain Shiganori Kami conceived a spectacular, one-way suicide mission by superbattleship *Yamato* and the Second Destroyer Squadron to attack the US invasion fleet. The toxic Kami then successfully isolated and sold the operation to Combined Fleet commander Admiral Soemu Toyoda during a closeted, all-night *sake* session. The next morning, with Toyoda's silent acquiescence, Kami unilaterally announced the decision to a stunned Combined Fleet staff. No one believed there was a realistic chance of operational success, but Kami was unconcerned, as he intended the *Yamato* sortie entirely to save face. Kami and Toyoda's surface attack mission was codenamed *Ten-Ichi-Go* (Operation *Heaven Number One*) and the assigned *Yamato* flotilla was euphemistically designated the "Surface Special Attack Force." *Ten-Ichi-Go's* vague, brief, and sloppily assembled mission orders off-handedly suggested that if *Yamato* reached Okinawa she were to beach herself as an artillery battery, while her men went ashore as naval infantry. No significant air cover was assigned. Ironically, had *Kikisui* No. 1 been delayed 24 hours to better coordinate with *Ten-Ichi-Go*, it would likely have prevented Mitscher's carriers from interfering with *Yamato's* approach.

The mission was bitterly opposed by many high-ranking IJN officers, who considered *Ten-Ichi-Go* a pointless waste of precious lives and resources merely to serve IJN vanity. When told the mission's purpose was "the tradition and glory of the Navy," Captain Atsushi Oi exclaimed, "This war is of our nation and why should the honor of our 'surface fleet' be more respected?

A brand-new *Yamato* races through the Bungo Strait during sea trials, October 20, 1941. As "Yamato" is an ancient, poetic name for Japan itself, the symbolism behind *Yamato*'s defiant but impossible eleventh-hour sortie against overwhelming American power is obvious. (NHHC NH 73092)

An undated 1945 image of four old US battleships in battle line, with Spruance's flagship *New Mexico* in the foreground, followed by her sister *Idaho* and then *Tennessee* on the far left. Had *Yamato* run into Deyo's battle line, she would have faced a combination of sixty 14in. and 16in. barrels, with 120 radar-directed heavy shells a minute landing on and around her. *Yamato* would have been mission-killed in minutes. However, *Yamato*'s 18.1in. shells could reliably penetrate the US battleships' armor. A few lucky magazine hits and *Yamato* might very well have taken one or two old US battleships with her. (NHHC 80-G-K-3706)

Who cares about their glory? Damn fools!" Among the dissenters, however quietly, was the mission's assigned commander, IJN Second Fleet's Vice Admiral Seiichi Ito. Nevertheless, as Rear Admiral Toshitane Takata admitted, some cold logic did underlie the operation: "[*Ten-Ichi-Go*] was the very last possible sortie we could have made from a viewpoint of fuel, personnel, and so on, that was our last gasp."

The relevant ship captains were assembled aboard light cruiser *Yahagi* and finally briefed on the mission on April 5. While hardly afraid to die, the officers were aghast at such a nakedly futile plan concocted by superiors with apparently no interest in success. They unanimously objected, with *Yahagi*'s Captain Tameichi Hara likening it to "throwing an egg against a rock." Ito's veteran officers pleaded to be allowed to independently raid US supply lines instead, which offered some hope of success, but the inexperienced Ito refused. Ito's officers then urged a direct, high-speed dash that would at least give the Americans less time to react, but Ito again refused, explaining he planned to steer wide around to the northwest of Okinawa in the hopes of confusing the Americans. That evening, Ito's captains disembarked as many nonessential personnel as possible before departure, *Yahagi*'s Hara explaining later, "The idea of herding 1,000 men to certain death did not appeal to me."

Late that night, Okinawa's Lieutenant-General Ushijima received an IJN message urging Ushijima's 32nd Army to counterattack the following day, April 6, to coincide with *Ten-Ichi-Go* and *Kikisui* No. 1. Ushijima found both *Ten-Ichi-Go* and the IJN's sudden demand to counterattack preposterous. He refused the order and demanded *Ten-Ichi-Go* be canceled.

Meanwhile, unknown to the Japanese, US intelligence had long broken Combined Fleet codes and was reading its transmissions. By April 5, Nimitz's Pacific intelligence office (JICPOA) had already divined the *Ten-Ichi-Go* mission and timetable to exquisite detail, even that *Yamato* would arrive off Okinawa at 0500hrs, April 8. Shortly after midnight, April 6, Spruance ordered Fifth Fleet to prepare to receive *Yamato*.

Hours later, the *Yamato* force departed Mitajiri anchorage to fuel at the IJN's Tokuyama depot. Toyoda had directed the *Yamato* force be fueled only enough for a one-way mission, but Tokuyama port workers covertly loaded the task force with additional fuel, perhaps enough to return home. Having taken 3,400 tons of fuel oil aboard, *Yamato* weighed anchor at 1524hrs, April 6, accompanied by Rear Admiral Keizo Komura's Second Destroyer Squadron (*Yahagi* and eight destroyers). Within 45 minutes a B-29 had spotted them underway. Submarine *Threadfin* (SS-410) then sighted the *Yamato* force transiting the Bungo Strait at 1745hrs and transmitted a contact report, which *Yamato* intercepted. A more detailed *Threadfin* report followed

Operation *Ten-Ichi-Go*, April 6–7, 1945

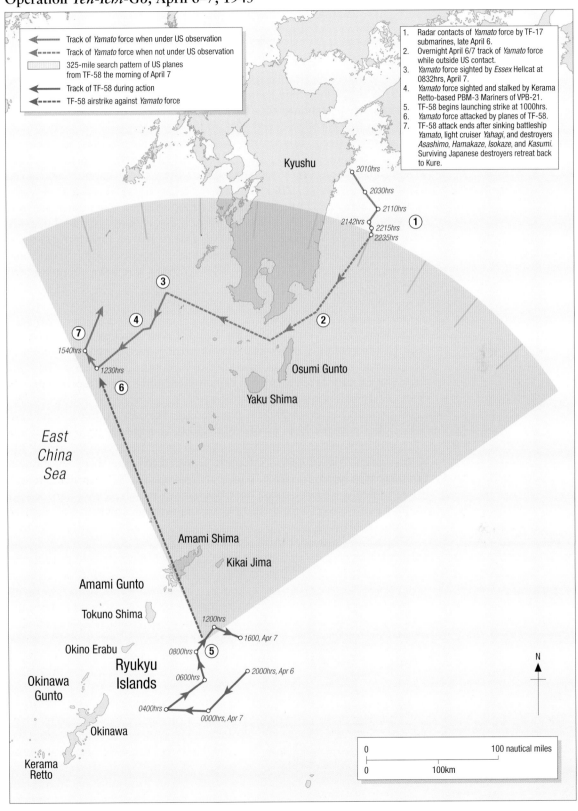

Track of *Yamato* force when under US observation

Track of *Yamato* force when not under US observation

325-mile search pattern of US planes from TF-58 the morning of April 7

Track of TF-58 during action

TF-58 airstrike against *Yamato* force

1. Radar contacts of *Yamato* force by TF-17 submarines, late April 6.
2. Overnight April 6/7 track of *Yamato* force while outside US contact.
3. *Yamato* force sighted by *Essex* Hellcat at 0832hrs, April 7.
4. *Yamato* force sighted and stalked by Kerama Retto-based PBM-3 Mariners of VPB-21.
5. TF-58 begins launching strike at 1000hrs.
6. *Yamato* force attacked by planes of TF-58.
7. TF-58 attack ends after sinking battleship *Yamato*, light cruiser *Yahagi*, and destroyers *Asashimo*, *Hamakaze*, *Isokaze*, and *Kasumi*. Surviving Japanese destroyers retreat back to Kure.

Kyushu

2010hrs
2030hrs
2110hrs
2142hrs
2215hrs
2235hrs
①

②

③

④

⑦
1540hrs
1230hrs
⑥

Osumi Gunto

Yaku Shima

East China Sea

Amami Shima
Kikai Jima

Amami Gunto

Tokuno Shima

1200hrs
1600, Apr 7

Okino Erabu
0800hrs ⑤

Ryukyu Islands
0600hrs
2000hrs, Apr 6

Okinawa Gunto
0400hrs
0000hrs, Apr 7

Okinawa

Kerama Retto

N

0   100 nautical miles

0   100km

at 2144hrs. As Ito's force rounded Kyushu to the southwest, it was shadowed overnight by submarine *Hackleback* (SS-295), which radioed four additional contact reports and was three times briefly pursued by one of *Yamato*'s escorting destroyers.

Fearing a repeat of April 6's mass *Kikisui*, Spruance ordered Mitscher's carriers to focus on repulsing Japanese air attacks, and instead ordered Deyo's TF-54 to intercept *Yamato*. Deyo's staff thrashed out a battle plan for the old, slow Standard-type battleships *Idaho*, *New Mexico*, *Tennessee*, *West Virginia*, *Maryland*, and *Colorado* to intercept the *Yamato* group, taking care to keep between the 27kt *Yamato* and the US transports off Okinawa. Despite persistent myth, by April 1945 Deyo's officers were fully aware *Yamato* exceeded 60,000 tons and mounted 18.1in. guns that ranged 45,000yds. Deyo's six 20kt US battleships would be escorted by seven modern cruisers and 21 destroyers. The Americans had four additional slow battleships available, *Arkansas*, *New York*, *Texas*, and *Nevada*, but these were early World War I relics too vulnerable to risk in a modern gunfight; the oldest, the 12in.-gunned *Arkansas*, had been commissioned in 1912. Even so, Deyo's newest battleship, *West Virginia*, had been commissioned in 1923.

Yamato's last stand, April 7

At 0620hrs, April 7, six Zeros of the 203rd Kokutai arrived over *Yamato* as CAP. Fourteen total Zeros would relay in small groups over the *Yamato* task force, but all would depart as scheduled by 1000hrs. The Americans already knew the exact CAP schedule of *Yamato*'s fighters, a later US intelligence memo dryly observing, "They left too soon."

At 0832hrs, an *Essex* Hellcat reported the *Yamato* task force southwest of Koshiki Retto at a heading of 300 degrees. The *Yamato* group was doing 22kts and deployed in a diamond formation, with *Yamato* in the center and *Yahagi* astern. *Yamato* simultaneously reported that she had been sighted. Visibility was highly variable, with patchy overcast. Within minutes, two VPB-21 PBM-3 Mariner flying boats (based at Kerama Retto with seaplane tender *Chandeleur*) arrived and began shadowing *Yamato* and radioing situation reports.

Meanwhile, Mitscher duly reported the *Yamato* sighting to Spruance, before dispatching 16 additional fighters at 0915hrs to track *Yamato*. To his chief-of-staff, Commodore Arleigh Burke, Mitscher announced: "Inform Admiral Spruance that I propose to strike the *Yamato* sortie group at 1200hrs unless otherwise directed." The grizzled aviator desperately wished to sink *Yamato*, but he likely suspected that Spruance, riding *New Mexico*, intended his beloved dreadnoughts claim one last moment of glory. "Will you take them or shall I?" Mitscher pressed. Spruance's response: "You take them."

At 1000hrs, Rear Admiral J.J. Jocko Clark's TG-58.1 and Rear Admiral Frederick "Ted" Sherman's TG-58.3 began launching their strike against the *Yamato*

A PBM Martin Mariner of FAW-1 alongside a seaplane tender at Kerama Retto. Mariners not only stalked the Japanese task force on April 7, but after *Yamato*'s sinking at least one Mariner would land and rescue a downed US airman and several Japanese survivors. (PhotoQuest/Getty Images)

task force. The two Task Groups' eight fast carriers combined to launch a first wave of 282 aircraft (132 fighters, 52 Helldiver dive-bombers, and 98 Avenger torpedo planes). However, TG-58.1's *Hancock* was 15 minutes late launching her strike of 53 planes. Saddled by poor visibility, *Hancock*'s strike ultimately never found *Yamato*. Rear Admiral Arthur Radford's TG-58.4 had just finished refueling and was rushing towards the launching area; Radford's attack would be late. Radford was additionally responsible for CAP over Okinawa, meaning TG-58.4 would ultimately contribute only 106 planes to the *Yamato* attack. The combined US first strike therefore came to 227 aircraft.

Riding battleship *Tennessee*, and still planning to fight *Yamato*, Deyo received a cheerful message from Turner: "Hope you will bring back a nice fish for breakfast." Deyo had begun writing his response on a message blank: "Many thanks, will try to ..." when word arrived that TF-58 was launching against *Yamato*. Deyo concluded: "... if the pelicans haven't caught them all!" *Yamato* never made it. Deyo would settle for forming history's last battle line against an approaching enemy.

The TF-58 strike flew north through moody, murky weather conditions towards *Yamato*'s reported location. *Essex*'s Lieutenant Thaddeus Coleman recalled, "We looked like a giant crop of blackbirds hunting for Farmer Ito's granary. The hunting got tougher and tougher. Clouds and more clouds. Rain and more rain ... Eventually it was like swimming through soup, we couldn't see a thing."

Yamato's CAP had either been unable or unwilling to engage the stalking Hellcats and departed on schedule at 1000hrs. Shortly afterwards, at 1014hrs, the Japanese discovered the two shadowing PBM-3 Mariners, and simultaneously reported a US submarine stalking the task force—this was *Hackleback*, which had managed to catch back up with the zig-zagging Japanese. Three minutes later, at 1017hrs, *Yamato* turned towards the Mariners and opened fire with her awesome 18.1in. *Sanshikidan* antiaircraft shells. *Yahagi* also opened fire, and additionally began jamming the Mariners' transmissions. The Mariners retreated into the clouds unharmed at 1018hrs, and *Yamato* and *Yahagi* ceased fire.

At 1107hrs, *Yamato*'s Type 13 air search radar detected a large formation inbound at 63nm, inspiring Ito to increase speed to 25kts. Within eight minutes the formation had closed to 44nm, prompting the Japanese to begin sharp evasive maneuvers. *Yamato* also received a delayed report from a Kikaigashima island observation post that 150 US planes were headed towards her.

Bennington's Lieutenant-Commander Hugh Woods' airborne radar detected the *Yamato* task force some 25nm away from its predicted location, and the US strike altered course. Five minutes later, the Americans made visual contact through a hole in the patchy 3,000ft overcast, a *Hornet* pilot recalling, "*Yamato* looked like the Empire State Building plowing through the water." *Yamato* cruised in the center, flanked by destroyers *Kasumi*, *Suzutsuki*, *Hamakaze*, and *Yukikaze*. Light cruiser *Yahagi* was in the van, followed by destroyers *Hatsushimo*, *Isokaze*, and *Fuyutsuki*. Captain Kotaki's division flagship, destroyer *Asashimo*, had begun suffering machinery problems five hours earlier and had fallen 12nm behind the main task force, to the north. At 1210hrs *Asashimo* radioed that she was under attack by enemy aircraft.

A Curtiss SB2C Helldiver overflies the burning *Yamato* and an escorting destroyer on April 7, 1945. The low overcast prevented the dive-bombers' preferred diving attacks from an altitude of 15,000ft. Instead, the Americans were forced to execute shallow glide bomb attacks from below 3,000ft, which would account for the relatively low number of bomb hits on *Yamato*. (Corbis via Getty Images)

Early in the battle and still maneuvering violently, *Yamato* narrowly avoids a US carrier plane's bomb just to port. *Yamato* is already smoking heavily from her after 6.1in. turret fire. Watching the US air attacks unfold aboard *Yamato*, Ito's chief-of-staff, Rear Admiral Morishita, commented, "Beautifully done, isn't it?" (NHHC L42-09.06.05)

San Jacinto's seven Hellcats dove against *Asashimo*, but the crippled destroyer threw up notably heavy flak. The Hellcats' 1,000lb bombs closely straddled *Asashimo*, buckling the destroyer's hull plating. The Hellcats then repeatedly strafed the destroyer, causing large fires that quickly silenced *Asashimo*'s guns. *San Jacinto*'s eight Avengers then made a textbook attack run at 300ft, dropping torpedoes from 1,200 to 1,600yds range. Trailing a wide oil slick, the crippled *Asashimo* attempted to comb the torpedoes, but one struck beneath her bridge and a second hit near her engine room. Successive explosions blew *Asashimo* partly out of the water and broke her in half. *Asashimo* sank at 1213hrs, going down with all 330 men. She had lasted three minutes against *San Jacinto*'s attack.

Twelve miles ahead, *Yamato* lookouts sighted the incoming US aircraft at 1232hrs. Unmolested by Japanese fighters, the US strike spent the next five minutes orbiting in multiple circles just outside Japanese antiaircraft range as the American commanders calmly organized a strike plan against the multiplicity of targets. About this time, and perhaps inevitably, *Yamato* hoisted Togo's legendary Tsushima flag signal: "*On this one battle rests the fate of our nation. Let every man do his utmost.*" Taking the intercom, Captain Ariga announced: "This is the commanding officer speaking. Stand by to repel air attacks. The decisive battle has begun."

At 1234hrs, *Yamato*'s two forward 18.1in. turrets opened *Sanshikidan* fire. A minute later *Yamato*'s entire antiaircraft battery erupted—nine 18.1in. rifles, twenty-four 127mm guns, and 152 25mm pom-poms. By all accounts, the Japanese antiaircraft fire was thick and visually dazzling. US Helldivers and Avengers responded by dumping "Window," thousands of 18in.-long aluminum streamers to jam Japanese gun-laying radar.

Ugaki's Fifth Air Fleet received *Yamato*'s desperate transmissions that she was under attack, a later report observing dryly, "It seems our [*Kikisui*] attacks had not completely shaken the enemy task forces." Ugaki's staff lamely washed its hands of the unfolding *Ten-Ichi-Go* disaster, explaining, "We were completely helpless to send emergency units to help the Surface Special Attack Force, for our entire strength was engaged at this time in assaulting the enemy task forces."

At 1237hrs, the circling US planes launched their coordinated attack against *Yamato* and her escorts. They had learned from the 1944 *Musashi* attacks, when *Yamato*'s sister ship had absorbed 16 bombs and 15 torpedoes before succumbing. This time, the Americans would concentrate their attacks against *Yamato*'s port side in the hopes of making her capsize.

Yamato was maneuvering hard at her flank speed of 27kts, when at 1240hrs four

Bennington Helldivers from VB-82 delivered two 1,000lb bombs near *Yamato*'s mainmast. The first bomb exploded in *Yamato*'s crew quarters. The second detonated near *Yamato*'s aft command station and caused serious damage, destroying one of *Yamato*'s two air search radars, her after secondary gun director, and several 25mm antiaircraft guns. The subsequent fires shortly reached the powder handling area beneath *Yamato*'s after 6.1in. turret and detonated the ready-use propellant. The resulting conflagration virtually exterminated the 6.1in. turret crew, but flash doors prevented the explosion from reaching the rest of the magazine. Nevertheless, the explosion killed the area's entire damage control party, meaning the resulting fire would rage uncontrolled for the rest of the battle. The Americans lost one Helldiver.

Dead in the water, the hapless light cruiser *Yahagi* is bracketed by multiple US bomb explosions. At 6,652 tons, *Yahagi* was virtually unarmored and less than one-tenth *Yamato*'s size, but she nevertheless absorbed a staggering amount of damage before succumbing—12 bombs and seven torpedoes. (NHHC 80-G-316084)

Meanwhile, US fighters repeatedly strafed *Yamato* with their 5in. rockets and 0.50cal. machine guns, decimating Japanese antiaircraft batteries and slaughtering exposed antiaircraft crews. The intense carnage and chaos that followed suppressed careful targeting and further ravaged Japanese gunners' morale.

At 1243hrs, eight *Hornet* Avengers launched torpedo attacks against *Yamato*'s port side, covered by 14 *Bunker Hill* Corsairs strafing *Yamato* with rockets. Antiaircraft fire hit six Avengers, destroying one, but at least three torpedoes hit the water. The first two torpedoes missed, but at 1245hrs the third torpedo slammed into *Yamato*'s port side, opening her hull to 2,235 tons of seawater. Japanese damage control counterflooded with 604 tons of water to correct the list.

Attempting to draw US attackers from *Yamato*, Hara's light cruiser *Yahagi* had maneuvered away from the Japanese battleship, steaming hard at 35kts. US strafing had already ricocheted machine gun bullets around *Yahagi*'s bridge, killing a lookout. Watching the attack unfold, Hara admitted, "The spectacle was at once thrilling and terrifying." Meanwhile, *Bennington*'s Lieutenant-Commander Ed De Garmo led three Avengers against *Yahagi*. At 1246hrs, De Garmo's Avengers delivered *Yahagi* her first hit—and it was a devastating one. A single torpedo struck *Yahagi* in the engine room, killing the entire engineering crew. *Yahagi* was left dead in the water nine minutes into the battle. Destroyer *Isokaze* subsequently sped towards *Yahagi* to take off Rear Admiral Komura.

About 56 US aircraft (34 fighters and 22 bombers) concentrated on *Yamato*'s escorting destroyers. *Hamakaze* quickly suffered a near-miss which disabled her starboard shaft. Then at 1247hrs, multiple torpedo hits blew *Hamakaze* in two. Long before she could reach *Yahagi*, *Isokaze* was hammered by US bombs. *Fuyutsuki* received superficial damage from two dud 5in. rockets, but *Suzutsuki* took a 500lb bomb that blew her bow off.

The first US attack ended at 1250hrs. *Yamato* had taken multiple hits, but still maintained 27kts. *Yamato* turned about to assess *Yahagi*'s condition. The battered cruiser could no longer make headway, and she began drifting

YAMATO'S LAST STAND, EAST CHINA SEA, APRIL 7, 1945 (PP.62–63)

Yamato (**1**), the world's greatest battleship, is seen a few minutes into her last battle at 1245hrs, April 7, 1945. Steaming hard at her flank speed of 27kts, *Yamato* and her nine escorts have just fallen under attack by Task Force 58's first wave of 227 US planes. Just moments earlier *Yamato* suffered her first damage when *Bennington* Helldivers planted two 1,000lb armor-piercing bombs amidships. The resulting fires, immediately aft of *Yamato*'s mainmast and nearly atop her after 6.1in. turret, will rage the rest of the battle.

TBM Avengers (**2**), from *Hornet*'s VT-17, are making their torpedo runs against *Yamato*. During this initial attack wave, the Americans score their first torpedo hit against *Yamato*'s portside hull. By 1945 the Americans' notoriously poor Mark 13 aerial torpedo had been greatly improved and was armed with a 600lb Torpex warhead, which was 50 percent more powerful than TNT.

Most of *Yamato*'s antiaircraft battery is still intact, most conspicuously her nine huge 460mm (18.1in.) main guns (**3**). They are firing specially designed *Sanshikidan* (Type 3) antiaircraft shells at the Americans. Weighing 2,998lbs, each 460mm *Sanshikidan* shell was filled with 966 incendiary tubes and 600 steel stays. A 460mm *Sanshikidan* shell's time-delay fuze was usually set to detonate one second after leaving the muzzle, which translates to 1,000m (1,100yds). Upon detonation, each *Sanshikidan* round was designed to burst into 2,846 fragments. These were thrown forward in a 20-degree-wide cone. Each of the 966 incendiary tubes would emit, for five seconds, a 16ft-long, 5,400-degree F flame. A *Sanshikidan* shell was theoretically effective up to 3,000yds forward from its burst, or 4,100yds from *Yamato*. But although the *Sanshikidan* blasts made a spectacular display on April 7, 1945, they proved completely ineffective against the attacking US aircraft.

behind the main task force. The brief interlude soon ended as *Yamato*'s surviving air search radar detected inbound aircraft four minutes out. This second attack comprised 50 US planes from *Essex* and *Bataan* (TG-58.3). At 1322hrs, an *Essex* Corsair scored against *Yamato*'s port bow with a 1,000lb high-explosive bomb. Twelve Helldivers nevertheless claimed multiple bomb hits near *Yamato*'s bridge, although Japanese antiaircraft fire damaged five Helldivers.

At 1333hrs the third wave of US attackers arrived, comprising 110 new *Yorktown*, *Intrepid*, and *Langley* aircraft from the delayed TG-58.4 strike. The Americans now overwhelmingly focused on the reeling *Yamato*. Twenty Avengers attacked *Yamato*'s portside. Around 1337hrs, the third wave saw three confirmed torpedo hits on *Yamato*'s portside, plus a fourth probable hit, increasing her portside list to 15–16 degrees. Stationed on *Yamato*'s bridge, Ensign Mitsuru Yoshida recalled, "I could hear the Captain vainly shouting, 'Hold on men! Hold on men!'"

Ariga had no option but to flood *Yamato*'s starboard machinery spaces, where hundreds of engineers toiled to keep *Yamato* underway. Yoshida described: "Water, both from torpedo hits and the flood valves rushed into these compartments and snuffed out the lives of the men at their posts, several hundred in all. Caught between cold sea water and steam and boiling water from the damaged boilers, they simply melted away." Ariga's drastic measure reduced *Yamato*'s portside list back to five degrees, but exhausted her last starboard counterflooding capacity. Having lost one shaft and gained 3,000 tons more water, *Yamato*'s speed fell to 12kts.

At 1342hrs, TG-58.4 Avengers dropped another four torpedoes. "That these pilots repeated their attacks with such accuracy and coolness," Yoshida marveled, "was a sheer display of the unfathomable, undreamed-of strength of our foes!" *Yamato* shot down one Avenger, but two torpedoes plowed into *Yamato*'s portside, making five torpedo hits in five minutes. The Americans had intentionally targeted *Yamato*'s stern to wreck her steering, and the gamble paid off. *Yamato*'s rudders were now disabled, jamming her in a permanent starboard turn. Any chance of reaching Okinawa was gone.

Reduced to 8kts and unable to maneuver, the dying *Yamato* made an easy target. Around 1402hrs, Mitscher's remorseless carrier planes now scored at least four more bomb hits, knocking out most of *Yamato*'s last functioning 25mm antiaircraft guns. *Yamato*'s wireless room had long since flooded, killing all transmissions. *Yamato*'s executive officer reported that counterflooding could no longer correct *Yamato*'s list and that all damage control officers were dead anyway. *Yamato* was stuck circling helplessly, still over 300nm north of Okinawa and beginning to sink. The mission was clearly a shambles and at 1402hrs Ito signaled via flag hoist that *Ten-Ichi-Go* was canceled. All Japanese warships that still could were to rescue survivors and attempt to escape back to Japan. Ariga ordered his crew to abandon ship. *Yamato*'s men duly removed the Emperor's portrait before allowing themselves to flee.

Throughout the battle, a stoic Ito had sat silently with arms crossed on *Yamato*'s

Reduced to 10–15kts, a reeling *Yamato*, burning aft and visibly listing to port, struggles late in the battle. She was photographed from a *Yorktown* Avenger, supposedly during the final decisive torpedo run. The world's greatest battleship has mere minutes to live. (NHHC NH 62580)

YAMATO'S LAST BATTLE, APRIL 7, 1945

Shown here are the TF-58 strikes that sank the
superbattleship *Yamato*.

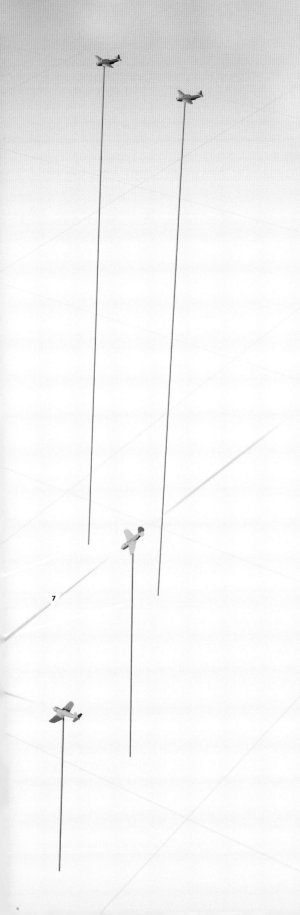

JAPANESE
IJN FIFTH AIR FLEET (UGAKI)
203rd Kokutai
***TEN-ICHI-GO* (ITO)**
Superbattleship *Yamato* (Ariga)
Second Destroyer Squadron
    (Komura)
Light cruiser *Yahagi* (Hara)
Destroyer *Fuyutsuki*
Destroyer *Yukikaze*
Destroyer *Hatsushimo*
Destroyer *Asashimo*
Destroyer *Kasumi*
Destroyer *Isokaze*
Destroyer *Hamakaze*

ALLIED
US TASK FORCE 58 (MITSCHER)
Task Group 58.1 (Clark)
CV-12 *Hornet* (CVG-17)
CV-18 *Bennington* (CVG-82)
CVL-24 *Belleau Wood* (CVLG-30)
CVL-30 *San Jacinto* (CVLG-45)
Task Group 58.3 (Sherman)
CV-9 *Essex* (CVG-4)
CV-17 *Bunker Hill* (CVG-84)
CV-19 *Hancock* (CVG-7)
CVL-28 *Cabot* (CVLG-29)
CVL-29 *Bataan* (CVLG-47)
Task Group 58.4 (Radford)
CV-10 *Yorktown* (CVG-3)
CV-11 *Intrepid* (CVG-10)
CVL-27 *Langley* (CVLG-23)
CVL-22 *Independence* (CVLG-46)
US TASK FORCE 54 (DEYO)
BB-43 *Tennessee*
BB-42 *Idaho*
BB-40 *New Mexico*
BB-48 *West Virginia*
BB-46 *Maryland*
BB-45 *Colorado*
7 cruisers
21 destroyers
US FLEET AIRWING ONE
VPB-21 (Two PBM-3 Mariners)
US TASK FORCE 112
SS-410 *Threadfin*
SS-295 *Hackleback*

EVENTS

(Note: event nos. 1, 2, 6, 8, and 14 do not refer directly to the diagram and so are not marked on it.)

April 7, 1945

1.   1232hrs: *Yamato* spots the first US attack wave of 227 aircraft, bearing 25 degrees to port at a range of 4,375yds.

2.   1234hrs: *Yamato*'s forward guns open fire on the US planes.

3.   1235hrs: *Yamato* increases speed to 24kts and engages her full antiaircraft battery, including all nine 18.1in. guns firing *Sanshikidan* shells. Two minutes later US planes begin their first attacks, including strafing runs at *Yamato*'s bridge.

4.   1240hrs: Attacking from port, four VB-82 Helldivers from *Bennington* dive on *Yamato*, now maneuvering at 27kts, and turning to starboard. *Yamato* takes two 1,000lb AP bombs near her mainmast, knocking out an air search radar, a secondary battery director, and several antiaircraft guns, but also igniting propellant for *Yamato*'s after 6.1in. turret. The blaze is impossible to put out. One Helldiver is shot down.

5.   1243hrs: Eight *Hornet* Avengers commence torpedo runs from *Yamato*'s port side, bearing 70 degrees. Three torpedoes hit the water. *Yamato* again turns hard to starboard, but she is struck by one torpedo at 1245hrs. The Japanese shoot down one Avenger. The first US attack ends at 1250hrs.

6.   1306hrs: The second US attack wave of 50 *Essex* and *Bataan* planes arrive.

7.   1322hrs: An *Essex* Corsair scores a 1,000lb high-explosive bomb hit against *Yamato*'s port bow.

8.   1333hrs: The third US wave of 110 *Yorktown*, *Intrepid*, and *Langley* aircraft arrive from TG-58.4.

9.   1337hrs: Twenty TG-58.4 Avengers make their torpedo runs from a bearing of 60 degrees off *Yamato*'s portside. *Yamato* turns hard into the torpedoes, but at least three and possibly four torpedoes slam into her, causing a 15–16 degree port list. Captain Ariga is forced to counterflood *Yamato*'s starboard machinery spaces. This reduces *Yamato*'s list back to five degrees, but she has absorbed an additional 3,000 tons of water. *Yamato*'s speed falls to 12kts.

10.   1342hrs: Four TG-58.4 Avengers make attack runs against *Yamato*'s port side, and two more torpedoes hit *Yamato*, jamming *Yamato* in a permanent starboard turn. One Avenger is shot down.

11.   1402hrs: US planes hit *Yamato* with at least four more bombs in quick succession.

12.   1407hrs: Setting their torpedoes' running depth for 20ft, Lieutenant Thomas Stetson's six Avengers deliberately target *Yamato*'s unarmored starboard side, high out of the water. *Yamato* takes her seventh torpedo hit.

13.   1417hrs: *Yamato* takes her eighth and ninth torpedoes in her port side.

14.   1420hrs: *Yamato* begins capsizing to port, her main deck vertical to the ocean. At 1423hrs *Yamato* slips beneath the East China Sea, then immediately explodes.

Yamato explodes in the East China Sea. "It made a mighty big bang," reported a Hellcat pilot. "Smoke went up—the fireball was about 1,000ft high." The detonation produced a 20,000ft-high mushroom cloud and was reportedly felt 110nm away in Kyushu. (NHHC NH 62582)

bridge, unflinching as bullets ricocheted around him, slaughtering his staff. Yoshida now observed that Ito "struggled to his feet. His chief of staff then arose and saluted. A prolonged silence followed during which they regarded each other solemnly." Ito then told his staff, "Save yourselves. I shall stay with the ship." Ito then shook hands deliberately with his officers, retired to his sea cabin one deck below, and locked it behind him.

Meanwhile, the Americans continued pummeling the helpless *Yahagi*, which "quivered and rocked as if made of paper," recalled Captain Hara. The stricken *Yahagi* suffered repeated hits. "My proud cruiser," Hara brooded, "was but a mass of junk, barely afloat." Around 1400hrs *Yahagi* took the decisive torpedo hit, triggering a clearly fatal starboard roll. Hara finally ordered, "Abandon ship." At 1405hrs, one minute after receiving her last bomb, *Yahagi* capsized and sank, having somehow absorbed at least 12 bombs and seven torpedoes. Captain Hara and Rear Admiral Komura calmly stepped into the water as *Yahagi* sank from beneath them, only barely surviving the sinking *Yahagi*'s undertow. Now clinging to floating wreckage, the exhausted Hara observed "scores of planes swarming about [*Yamato*] like gnats."

Having lost all power shortly after 1400hrs, *Yamato* was now lying nearly on her side, with her unarmored starboard side high out of the water. *Yorktown*'s Lieutenant-Commander Herbert Houk dispatched Lieutenant Thomas Stetson's division of six Avengers to deliver a final torpedo attack into the unarmored starboard keel. Stetson's men re-set their torpedoes for a running depth of 20ft and made their attack. At 1407hrs *Yamato* was struck in her exposed starboard side by a seventh torpedo.

At 1417hrs *Yamato* took her eighth and ninth torpedoes in her port side. Meanwhile, with *Yamato*'s pumps no longer functioning, alarms began to blare: temperatures in the 18.1in. magazines were approaching dangerous levels. By 1420hrs, the capsizing *Yamato*'s main deck was vertical to the ocean. Captain Ariga, eating a biscuit given to him by a rating, tied himself to a binnacle on *Yamato*'s bridge. As *Yamato* capsized, surviving men clambered across her keel, a crazed, half-naked officer screaming and brandishing his samurai sword at the Americans.

At 1423hrs, just after *Yamato* slipped beneath the East China Sea, the sinking dreadnought exploded catastrophically. *Yamato*'s capsizing motion had likely forced open her 18.1in. powder room doors, allowing fires into the battleship's magazines. An American gunner described the explosion as "the prettiest sight I've ever seen … A red column of fire shot up through the clouds and when it faded *Yamato* was gone." The detonation killed most *Yamato* survivors still struggling in the water and may have destroyed several US aircraft. The Americans' exact score will never be known, but *Yamato* had certainly absorbed seven bombs and nine to twelve torpedoes out of 150 torpedoes dropped. The US planes departed at 1443hrs, but not before issuing "a few farewell strafing runs across the *Yamato* survivors."

Destroyers *Suzutsuki*, *Fuyuzuki*, *Yukikaze*, and *Hatsushimo* rescued 1,620 men from the original task force (including Hara and Komura) before successfully escaping back to Japan. Destroyers *Asashimo* and *Hamakaze* had sunk in action, while the disabled *Isokaze* and *Kasumi* were scuttled by *Yukikaze* and *Fuyuzuki*. *Yahagi* and the Japanese destroyers had suffered 1,187 dead. Of *Yamato*'s 3,332 crew, just 267 were saved; they included Yoshida and his priceless account of *Yamato*'s bridge. Combined losses for *Ten-Ichi-Go* were 4,242 Japanese killed. Upon learning *Yamato*'s fate, Okinawa's Lieutenant-General Ushijima could only react with disgust. "What an infernal waste! I advised the navy not to try it!" Years later, an American historian would observe less prosaically: "If the story of the shift of power at sea from once-mighty dreadnoughts to aircraft carriers needed a final chapter, it was written that afternoon as *Yamato* went down."

KIKISUI NO. 2, APRIL 12–13

Seeking the fleeing remnants of the *Yamato* task force, on April 8 Mitscher launched a futile 32-fighter search out to 325nm. Meanwhile, perhaps cheered by *Yamato*'s demise, Turner messaged Nimitz: "I may be crazy but it looks like the Japs have quit the war, at least in this section." Nimitz signaled back, "Delete all after 'crazy'!" That evening, three kamikazes attacked destroyer *Gregory* (DD-802) at RPS-3 north of Okinawa. The first crashed into *Gregory* but the last two were shot down. Suffering two wounded, *Gregory* steamed to Kerama Retto for repairs.

The following evening, April 9, four kamikazes attacked RPS-4 northeast of Okinawa. One crashed destroyer *Sterrett* (DD-407), forcing her to retire. That same day, a suicide boat out of Naha rammed destroyer *Charles J. Badger* (DD-657), knocking her out of the war. The Americans repulsed five additional suicide boats and 15 grenade-armed swimmers. Meanwhile, destroyer-transport *Hopping* (APD-51) was damaged dueling a Nakagusuku Wan shore battery, losing two dead and 18 wounded.

Superb American signals work again predicted Japanese attacks, with TF-58's April 11 report cryptically claiming, "All indications pointed to a busy day." Mitscher degassed and disarmed all bombers, stowed them below, and scrambled an overhead CAP of 84 fighters, while dispatching another 48 to help defend Okinawa. The expected attack commenced at 1130hrs and continued sporadically throughout the day. TF-58 fighters shot down 17 planes and flak claimed another 12, but numerous attackers got through.

Japanese aerial bombs damaged carrier *Essex* and destroyer *Hale* (DD-642), while Japanese strafing damaged destroyers *Black* (DD-666) and *Hank* (DD-702). That afternoon, a kamikaze crashed destroyer *Kidd* (DD-661), a TF-58 picket, killing 38 and wounding 55. Another Zero crashed battleship *Missouri*, inflicting superficial damage. Nine kamikazes fell within 100yds of TF-58 warships, with *Enterprise* moderately damaged by four near-misses.

In one of the war's most famous photographs, an impossibly low-flying kamikaze bores in on battleship *Missouri* just before impact, April 11, 1945. *Missouri*'s armored belt absorbed the plane with a small dent. The following day *Missouri*'s skipper, Captain William Callaghan, gave the 19-year-old Japanese pilot, Setsuo Ishino, a full military burial at sea, which proved highly unpopular with *Missouri*'s mostly conscripted crew. (NHHC NH 62696)

TF-51 radar picket stations off Okinawa during *Iceberg*

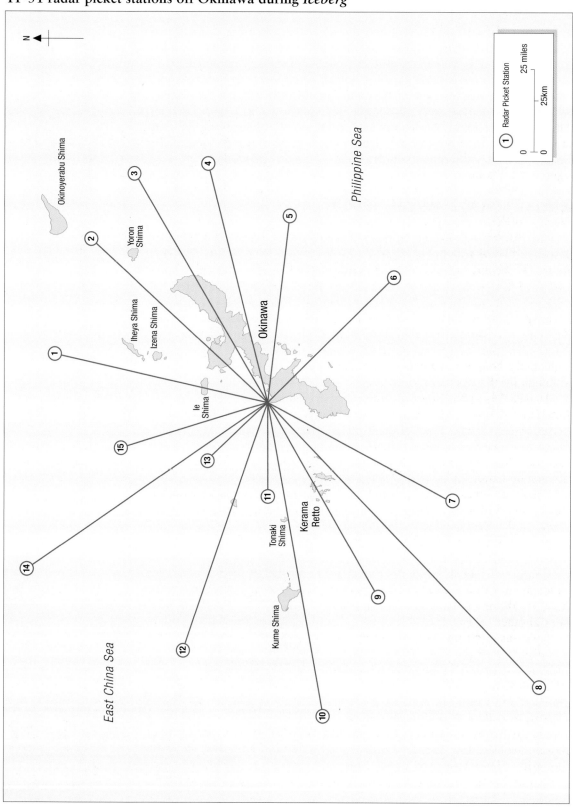

Enterprise, *Kidd*, and three additional destroyers detached to Ulithi for repairs. Small intermittent raids harassed TF-58 overnight, scoring no hits but losing 18 planes to TF-58 night fighters and antiaircraft fire.

Rainy weather delayed *Kikisui* No. 2 until April 12, when 380 Japanese planes (185 kamikazes) sortied almost entirely against TF-51 west of Okinawa. Forewarned by cryptanalysis, Turner exhorted scrambling US fighters: "Don't let any return." TF-58 fighter patrols north of Okinawa claimed 151 Japanese aircraft at the cost of just six of their own. TF-51 ships and CAPs shot down another 147 attackers, numbers that again proved insufficient.

Despite a barrage of heavy antiaircraft fire, battleship *Tennessee* was struck by a D3A Val while cruising off the Hagushi beaches, April 12, 1945. Just moments earlier, *Tennessee*'s escorting destroyer *Zellars* (DD-777) had been crashed by a B5N Kate. (NARA via WW2DB)

That afternoon several waves attacked RPS-1, with a Val crashing destroyer *Cassin Young* (DD-793) at 1346hrs and relegating her to Kerama Retto. A second raid at 1445hrs crashed destroyer *Purdy* (DD-734), *LCS(L)-57*, and *LCS(L)-33*, sinking the last one. RPS-1 suffered a combined 20 men killed and 121 wounded.

Despite attempting numerous missions, Kanoya's specially trained 721st Kokutai *Jinrai-Butai* ("Divine Thunder") unit had so far failed to launch a single *Ohka* suicide rocket against the Americans. On April 12, however, eight Betty bombers would finally launch six *Ohkas* against Fifth Fleet, although five Betties never returned.

At RPS-14, about 70nm northwest of Okinawa, a Zero plowed into *Mannert L. Abele* (DD-733)'s engine room at 1440hrs, its 500lb bomb exploding and leaving the destroyer dead in the water. One minute later an *Ohka* came screaming in at 575mph, slammed into *Mannert L. Abele* and exploded. She sank in five minutes, losing 97 dead. *Mannert L. Abele* was the first destroyer hit by an *Ohka* and the last sunk by one.

Destroyer-minesweeper *Jeffers* (DMS-27), en route to assist *Mannert L. Abele*, observed a twin-engined bomber eight miles away drop a smoking "belly tank" that suddenly rocketed towards *Jeffers* "at terrific speed." Numerous 40mm hits and hard maneuvering saw the *Ohka* miss *Jeffers* astern and disintegrate.

Charging to assist *Cassin Young*, RPS-2 destroyer *Stanly* (DD-478) was suddenly hit by an *Ohka* which tore completely through *Stanly*'s starboard bow, 5ft above the waterline, its warhead exploding close aboard. Minutes later another *Ohka* penetrated *Stanly*'s antiaircraft fire, ultimately ripping *Stanly*'s ensign from its gaff before bouncing wildly across the water and disintegrating.

A major attack unfolded against TG-54.1 off the Hagushi beaches. After battleship *Idaho* splashed four attacking kamikazes, a fifth exploded close aboard, wounding ten and causing extensive but noncritical damage. Destroyer *Zellars* (DD-777) shot down two attacking Jills but the third, repeatedly hit by antiaircraft fire, smashed into her, its bomb detonating. Simultaneously, five kamikazes attacked battleship *Tennessee*, steaming alongside. *Tennessee* shot down four, but the fifth doubled back into *Tennessee*'s signal bridge and careened aft, killing 25 and wounding 104. *Tennessee* remained in action. The crippled *Zellars* limped to Kerama Retto, her crew steering "via jury-rigged sound-powered telephone lines and … judicious profanity."

Kamikazes also heavily damaged destroyer-minelayer *Lindsey* (DM-32) and destroyer-escort *Whitehurst* (DE-634), with *Lindsey* losing 57 men dead and *Whitehurst* 42. Both successfully reached Kerama Retto. Patrolling for submarines at "Kamikaze Gulch," destroyer-escort *Rall* (DE-304) shot down three attackers but was crashed by a Ki-27 Nate that killed 21 and wounded 38. Kamikazes also damaged destroyer-escorts *Riddle* (DE-185) and *Walter C. Wann* (DE-412).

Late that night, intensely bright flares suddenly erupted above Deyo's battleships southwest of Okinawa, signaling a torpedo attack. Deyo ordered evasive action, and observed several torpedoes exploding harmlessly in the wakes of the hard-maneuvering battleships *Tennessee* and *Idaho*. However, the day's conventional air attacks had damaged light cruiser *Oakland*, destroyers *Norman Scott* (DD-690) and *Brush* (DD-745), and destroyer-escorts *Conklin* (DE-439) and *Damon E. Cummings* (DE-643).

Dawn, April 13 brought Fifth Fleet devastating news. Aboard carrier *Hornet*, Rear Admiral J.J. Jocko Clark personally woke Lieutenant-Commander John Roosevelt and handed him the unhappy dispatch. Roosevelt's father, President Franklin Delano Roosevelt, was dead. Clark offered to immediately transfer Roosevelt home. He refused: "My place is here." On Sunday, April 15, all Fifth Fleet ships, including the Royal Navy's, would hold a memorial service for the late president.

The war continued. The afternoon of April 14, 50 Japanese attackers fell to TF-58 fighters. Another 12 succumbed to TF-58 flak, including 10 to TF-58's radar pickets, who received most of the Japanese raid. However, TF-58 destroyer *Sigsbee* (DD-502) took a kamikaze aft that killed 23 men, wrecked *Sigsbee*'s steering, and cut speed to 5kts. *Sigsbee*'s skipper, Commander Gordon Pai'ea Chung-Hoon, continued directing *Sigsbee*'s antiaircraft fire and damage control efforts until *Sigsbee* was towed to safety. Fellow TF-58 destroyers *Dashiell* (DD-659) and *Hunt* (DD-674) were also slightly damaged by the raids. Finally, at 1930hrs an unidentified kamikaze crashed TF-54 battleship *New York* 15nm southeast of Nakagusuku Wan, wounding two and destroying a Kingfisher floatplane.

USMC antiaircraft fire lights up the night sky over American-occupied Yontan airfield, mid-April 1945. Marine Corsairs are visible in the foreground. A few squadrons of Japanese planes had been based at Okinawan airfields in March, but they were quickly destroyed before L-Day. (Corbis via Getty Images)

KIKISUI NO. 3, APRIL 16

Ugaki's staff conceded that *Kikisui* No. 2 had "suffered heavy losses." Nevertheless, *Ten-Go*'s third *Kikisui* was scheduled for April 16. Fifth Air Fleet admitted, "Unless this air superiority attack is carried out successfully, the antitask force attack on the enemy ships off Okinawa will not be carried off." Warned by intelligence, 125 TF-58 fighters preemptively struck Kyushu airfields on April 15, losing two but claiming 29 Japanese shot down and 118 destroyed or damaged on the ground.

TF-58's Kyushu sweeps the following day, April 16, claimed 55 additional Japanese planes destroyed and 79 damaged on the ground at Kyushu; TF-58 lost nine planes and six men. Nevertheless, at least 289 Japanese attackers sortied against Fifth Fleet in *Kikisui* No. 3, with 142 against TF-58 and at least 147 against TF-51. American CAPs claimed a combined 203 kills—the third-highest scoring day of the campaign. Yet despite 14 Japanese planes falling to TF-58 flak, a kamikaze crashed carrier *Intrepid*'s flight deck, killing eight and wounding 21. *Intrepid* eventually detached for repairs; her war was over.

US fast carrier *Intrepid* just after being hit by a kamikaze on April 16. This was *Intrepid*'s fourth kamikaze hit in the war. The unidentified plane slammed into *Intrepid*'s deck near her aft elevator before penetrating to the hangar deck and starting a fire. Three hours later *Intrepid* was landing planes, but she would be detached for repairs the following day. (NHHC 80-G-328511)

Dawn had found Commander Frederick Becton's destroyer *Laffey* (DD-724) patrolling RPS-1. *Laffey*'s radar was already reading inbound bogies at first light, and soon registered 50 separate attackers closing from the northern quadrant alone. *Laffey*'s executive officer, Lieutenant Challen McCune, watched the approaching blips. "They'll come, captain," McCune apprised Becton. "We'll have to hold the bastards off ourselves."

Laffey's ordeal began at 0827hrs. Attacked 22 times over the next 80 minutes, *Laffey* would survive six kamikaze crashes, four bomb hits, and numerous strafings, suffering 32 men killed and 71 wounded. *Laffey*'s gunners shot down nine Japanese aircraft, but eventually only four 20mm guns remained operational. Nevertheless, when a *Laffey* officer asked Commander Becton if they might have to abandon ship, Becton snapped, "No! I'll never abandon ship as long as a single gun will fire!" Under his breath, a nearby lookout added, "And if I can find one man to fire it."

Laffey's neighbors suffered their own attacks. *LST-51*, some 600yds off *Laffey*, shot down a Japanese plane attacking the battered destroyer, before exploding another just 25ft away that severely damaged the LST. Destroyer *Bryant* (DD-665), at RPS-2, had been rushing towards *Laffey*'s location when at 0934hrs six Japanese planes attacked her. One crashed the base of *Bryant*'s bridge, killing 34 and wounding 33. Six miles east of *Laffey*, a Val successfully crashed *LCS-116*, killing 12 and causing severe damage. Meanwhile, destroyer-minesweeper *Macomb* (DMS-23) took the battered *Laffey* in tow at 1247hrs, ending "the longest three hours ever experienced by all hands," according to Commander Becton.

At RPS-14, destroyer *Pringle* (DD-477) shot down two kamikazes before a third slammed into her and exploded. *Pringle* broke in two and sank in six minutes, losing 78 men. Destroyer-minesweeper *Harding* (DMS-28) was quickly dispatched to replace *Pringle*. She repulsed two kamikazes and destroyed a third, but a fourth crashed close aboard, its bomb exploding beneath *Harding*'s keel, killing 22 and wounding nine. *Harding* was towed to Kerama Retto but was never repaired.

By noon April 17, TF-58 fighters had claimed another 49 kills, while TF-58 antiaircraft fire splashed five more. One TF-58 plane was lost. Late that night, battleship *Missouri* sighted an enemy submarine 12nm away. The resulting hunter-killer operation by light carrier *Bataan* and four destroyers sank Japanese submarine *I-56*. In fact, *I-56* belonged to the *Tatara* group of four *Kaiten*-armed submarines the IJN had dispatched to attack Fifth Fleet back on March 28. The Americans had already repulsed *I-47* on March 29,

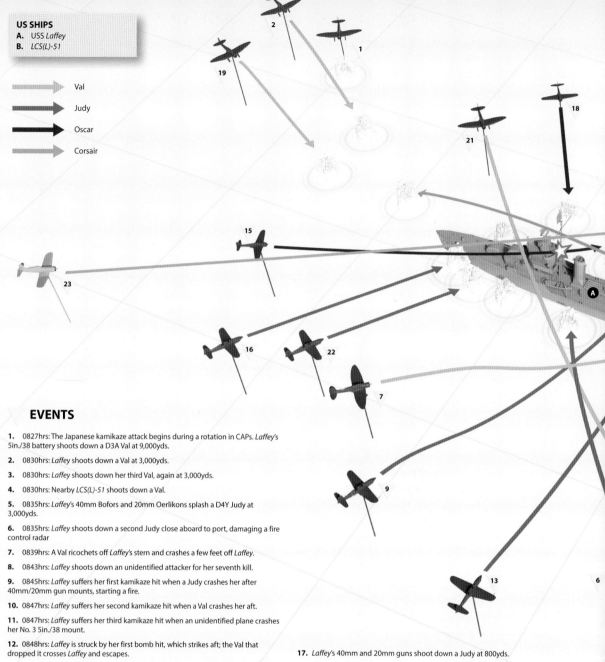

US SHIPS

A. USS *Laffey*
B. *LCS(L)-51*

Val

Judy

Oscar

Corsair

EVENTS

1. 0827hrs: The Japanese kamikaze attack begins during a rotation in CAPs. *Laffey's* 5in./38 battery shoots down a D3A Val at 9,000yds.

2. 0830hrs: *Laffey* shoots down a Val at 3,000yds.

3. 0830hrs: *Laffey* shoots down her third Val, again at 3,000yds.

4. 0830hrs: Nearby *LCS(L)-51* shoots down a Val.

5. 0835hrs: *Laffey's* 40mm Bofors and 20mm Oerlikons splash a D4Y Judy at 3,000yds.

6. 0835hrs: *Laffey* shoots down a second Judy close aboard to port, damaging a fire control radar

7. 0839hrs: A Val ricochets off *Laffey's* stern and crashes a few feet off *Laffey*.

8. 0843hrs: *Laffey* shoots down an unidentified attacker for her seventh kill.

9. 0845hrs: *Laffey* suffers her first kamikaze hit when a Judy crashes her after 40mm/20mm gun mounts, starting a fire.

10. 0847hrs: *Laffey* suffers her second kamikaze hit when a Val crashes her aft.

11. 0847hrs: *Laffey* suffers her third kamikaze hit when an unidentified plane crashes her No. 3 5in./38 mount.

12. 0848hrs: *Laffey* is struck by her first bomb hit, which strikes aft; the Val that dropped it crosses *Laffey* and escapes.

13. 0849hrs: *Laffey* suffers her fourth kamikaze hit when an unidentified plane crashes into her after deckhouse.

14. 0850hrs: *Laffey* suffers her fifth kamikaze hit when a second plane crashes her after deckhouse. *Laffey* has now suffered five kamikaze hits and one bomb hit in five minutes, causing flooding and fires aft and destroying her directors. *Laffey's* remaining antiaircraft guns are reduced to firing under local control.

15. 0850hrs–0945hrs: Because of the damage and chaos, the exact times of remaining events are in question, although their sequence is not. At 0850hrs, *Laffey's* replacement CAP—12 VMF-441 Corsairs—finally arrives overhead to the cheers of *Laffey's* battered survivors. They will claim 17 Japanese attackers. One of the Corsairs finds itself in hot pursuit of a Ki-43 Oscar fighter, which strikes *Laffey's* foremast and crashes to *Laffey's* starboard for *Laffey's* sixth kamikaze hit. However, the tightly pursuing Corsair has flown through *Laffey's* antiaircraft fire and is accidentally shot down. Its pilot bails out and is later rescued by *LCS(L)-51*.

16. *Laffey* suffers her second bomb hit, this time to her No. 2 5in./38 mount, but the Judy that dropped it is shot down by *Laffey's* CAP.

17. *Laffey's* 40mm and 20mm guns shoot down a Judy at 800yds.

18. *Laffey's* 5in./38 battery shoots down an Oscar at 500yds.

19. *Laffey's* No. 2 5in./38 mount shoots down a Val at 600yds.

20. *Laffey* suffers her third bomb hit when a Val, closing from astern, drops a bomb that hits *Laffey* aft, but is then shot down by *Laffey's* CAP.

21. *Laffey* suffers her fourth bomb hit when a Val crosses *Laffey* from her starboard bow, drops a bomb that hits a 20mm mount forward, and is then splashed by *Laffey's* CAP.

22. *Laffey's* antiaircraft fire and her CAP combine to shoot down a Judy.

23. At 0950hrs, some 24 additional USMC Corsairs and USN Hellcats roar overhead to reinforce *Laffey's* CAP. The Japanese attacks immediately end. Excellent ship-handling by *Laffey's* skipper, Commander Becton, means most of the serious damage has been taken aft, allowing *Laffey's* machinery (located amidships) to keep the destroyer powered throughout the battle. However, *Laffey's* rudder is jammed, and she is flooding and ablaze aft, with 31 crewmen dead and 72 wounded. Only four 20mm guns remain operational.

USS *LAFFEY* VERSUS THE KAMIKAZES, APRIL 16, 1945

Allen M. Sumner-class destroyer USS *Laffey* (DD-724) is attacked by 40–50 Japanese aircraft. *Laffey*'s antiaircraft battery comprises six 5in./38 DP guns, 12 40mm Bofors guns, and 11 20mm Oerlikon guns. Stationed 500–900yds to port of *Laffey* is *LCS(L)-51*, which is armed with six 40mm Bofors guns. *LCS(L)-51* will provide *Laffey* antiaircraft fire support throughout the action.

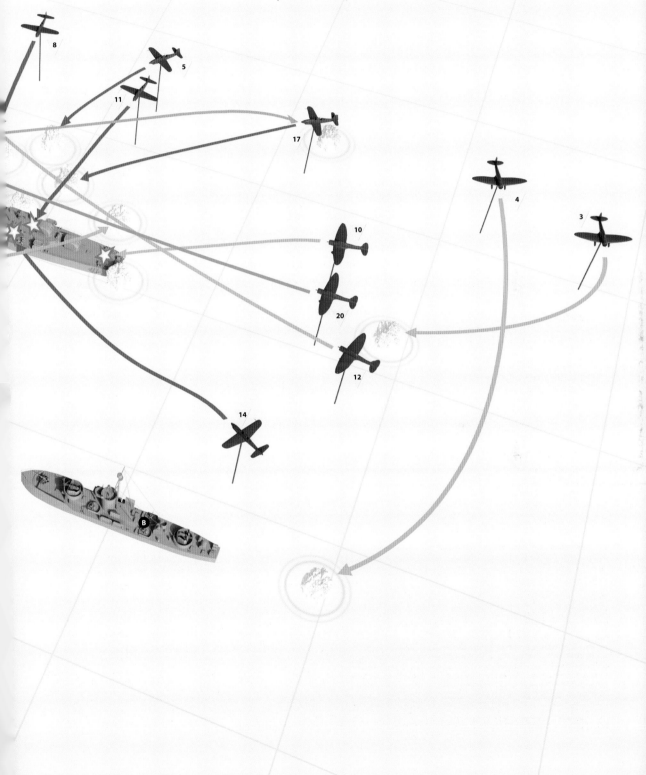

while the third, *I-44*, would be sunk by a *Tulagi* Avenger on April 29. The last submarine, *I-58*, would return home without engaging the Americans.

Rawlings' TF-57 strikes Formosa and the Sakishima Gunto, April 12–20

Following an April 8–9 replenishment, Spruance had unexpectedly requested TF-57 to attack the Shinchiku and Matsuyama airfields in northern Formosa. Rawlings enthusiastically agreed; TF-57 was now fulfilling Nimitz's earlier prediction that British carriers would be Fifth Fleet's "most flexible reserve." Poor weather canceled planned April 11 strikes, but at 0715hrs, April 12, TF-57 launched 48 Avengers and 40 fighters against Formosa's Shinchiku and Kiirun Harbor. TF-57 fighters claimed 16 Japanese planes; total British losses were three aircraft. That evening Rawlings delayed TF-57's scheduled Leyte-Samar retirement and volunteered Spruance an additional strike period against Sakishima Gunto. Spruance concurred, adding "This is fine initiative and cooperation." TF-57 struck Formosa again on April 13, repulsed four kamikazes, and then retired to replenish.

By April 14, carrier HMS *Formidable* had reached Rawlings' TF-57 from Leyte-Samar, allowing the long-battered *Illustrious* to withdraw for a major refit; *Illustrious'* war was over. On April 16–17, TF-57 hammered airfields across Sakishima Gunto, losing seven planes. TF-57 replenished on April 18, before launching unsolicited April 20 strikes that included rocket-armed Fireflies. TF-57 then retired for Leyte-Samar. In 12 days of action, Rawlings' carriers had flown 2,444 sorties, with 1,961 by fighters and 483 by Avengers. TF-57 aircraft had delivered 412 tons of bombs and 315 rockets, claimed 134 enemy planes in the air and on the ground, and sunk or severely damaged over 100 sampans and small vessels.

KIKISUI NO. 4, APRIL 27–28

By April 19, Ugaki had 598 planes available. He had deployed 1,406 total planes since March 23, with 668 coming from Fifth Air Fleet, 420 from Third Air Fleet, and 317 from Tenth Air Fleet, which only recently had been permanently withdrawn from *Ten-Go* operations. That morning, Tenth Army's XXIV Corps launched a major attack against the Shuri line. Beginning at 0540hrs, six old battleships, six cruisers, and six destroyers of Deyo's TF-54 began a bombardment of Japanese positions. Additionally, a TF-58 detachment of fast battleships— *Washington*, *North Carolina*, *South Dakota*, and DesRon-48—began a pre-dawn bombardment of Okinawa's south and southwest coasts. Another 650 USN and USMC planes bombed, rocketed, strafed, and napalmed the target area. The XXIV Corps attack lunged forward at 0640hrs but made virtually no progress over the next five days.

After a multi-day lull, the IJAAF alone resumed attacks on April 22, dispatching 41 combined planes from Kyushu and Formosa.

A 16in. salvo from fast battleship *North Carolina* hits Okinawa (date unknown). Permanently assigned to the fast carriers, the new, modern fast battleships had little chance to practice any shore bombardment skills. At Okinawa they were often used for diversions, while the more experienced slow battleships hammered the real targets. (WW2DB)

Ten VMF-323 Corsairs engaged at least 33 attackers, claiming 24.5 kills. Japanese planes nevertheless sank minesweeper *Swallow* (AM-65) and *LCS(L)(3)-15*, and damaged destroyers *Hudson* (DD-475), *Isherwood* (DD-520), and minesweeper *Ransom* (AM-283).

On April 27, a Japanese suicide boat successfully dropped a depth charge near destroyer *Hutchins* (DD-476), conducting gunfire support at Nakagusuku Bay. Suffering severe damage but no casualties, *Hutchins* limped to Kerama Retto and out of the war. Less successful was the *Tembu* group's submarine *I-36*, whose four *Kaitens* and subsequent conventional torpedo all missed a 28-ship LST/LSM convoy east of Okinawa.

The battered destroyer *Hazelwood* (DD-531), wrecked but still afloat, April 29, 1945. *Hazelwood* had been struck in the No. 2 stack by a diving Zero, which careened forward and destroyed *Hazelwood*'s bridge and most of her forward superstructure before exploding. (US Navy)

Meanwhile, *Kikisui* No. 4 commenced that evening, ending five straight days without air action. At 2125hrs, a kamikaze crashed and sank ammunition ship *Canada Victory* off Hagushi, killing three and wounding 12. Kamikazes had now sunk three fully loaded Victory ships, denying Tenth Army a combined 24,000 tons of munitions. Kamikazes additionally crashed destroyer *Ralph Talbot* (DD-390) and destroyer-transport *Rathburne* (APD-25).

The bulk of *Kikisui* No. 4's 115 kamikazes came on April 28. US fighters destroyed most, but seven kamikazes reached RPS-2 that afternoon. Destroyers *Daly* (DD-519) and *Twiggs* (DD-591) shot down five but were both damaged by near-misses. At 1930hrs an IJAAF kamikaze crashed evacuation transport *Pickney* (APH-2), anchored off Kerama Retto. *Pickney* suffered 34 dead. Late that night, after making several slow, low-level passes, an unidentified IJAAF fighter dove into fully lit hospital ship *Comfort* (AH-6) south of Okinawa, killing 28 (including six female nurses) and wounding 48. *Comfort* limped to Los Angeles for repairs. The following day, Zeros crashed destroyers *Hazelwood* (DD-531) and *Haggard* (DD-555), killing a combined 59 Americans, including *Hazelwood*'s skipper.

During April, US fighters claimed 1,216 air-to-air kills (937 USN and 279 USMC). Japanese sources admit combined IJNAF and IJAAF losses exceeded 1,000 planes, with 820 destroyed in the first four *Kikisui*. Over half of IJN Fifth Air Fleet had been destroyed—some 700 aircraft. Ugaki now had 620 aircraft, although only 370 were operational. But Ugaki's flyers had also scored heavily; Spruance reported USN casualties at 1,853 killed or missing and 2,650 wounded. As April expired, a concerned Nimitz personally visited Okinawa, where Buckner reminded Nimitz that as a land battle, Tenth Army operations fell under US Army command. "Yes," Nimitz replied, "but ground though it may be, I'm losing a ship and a half a day. So if this line isn't moving within five days, we'll get someone here to move it so we can all get out from under these stupid air attacks."

Nevertheless, by May, Tenth Army had thoroughly bogged down into costly, unimaginative frontal assaults against southern Okinawa's heavily fortified Shuri line. Numerous Tenth Army generals urged Buckner to "play the amphib card" and land the reserve 2nd Marine Division in southeastern

Okinawa, behind Japanese lines. Buckner ultimately refused, claiming insufficient logistics. Nimitz concurred with Buckner, at least publicly, but few others did.

Spruance, Turner, and Mitscher were themselves growing increasingly bitter at Tenth Army's lack of progress, as well as USAAF lethargy constructing fighter airfields ashore that could finally relieve the battered carriers. Touring the developing Okinawa airstrips, a Fifth Fleet staff officer discovered USAAF commander-in-chief General Henry "Hap" Arnold had secretly been writing Okinawa's lead USAAF engineer, urging him to divert assigned fighter strip resources into building B-29 bomber airfields instead. An incredulous Spruance went ashore to investigate and discovered the allegation was true. Stunned, Spruance "turned that situation around in about 15 minutes."

KIKISUI NO. 5, MAY 3–4

By May 2, IJN Fifth Air Fleet claimed: "The situation on Okinawa, at present, is such that our forces will be annihilated if a counterattack is not carried out." At IJA 32nd Army headquarters, a reluctant Ushijima allowed his reckless chief-of-staff, Major-General Isamu Cho, to talk him into just such a full-scale counterattack against Buckner's Tenth Army. Ugaki accordingly planned *Kikisui* No. 5 to support Cho's ill-advised Okinawa counteroffensive, scheduled for dusk, May 3.

Kikisui No. 5 began the afternoon of May 3, when at least 19 kamikazes sortied from Formosa. Three 17th Sentai Ki-61 Tonies attacked RPS-9 that evening. Two fell to flak, but the third crashed destroyer-minelayer *Macomb* (DMS-23) at 1830hrs, killing seven and wounding 14.

Some 26nm to the northwest, an estimated 20 kamikazes attacked RPS-10. At 1841hrs, destroyer-minelayer *Aaron Ward* (DM-34) suffered the first of five kamikaze hits that ultimately crippled her and killed 42. Two minutes later destroyer *Little* (DD-803) suffered four kamikaze hits in four minutes and quickly sank, suffering 31 killed and 79 wounded. Kamikazes also damaged *LCS(L)-25* and sank *LSM(R)-195*, totaling three ships sunk and 86 Americans killed at RPS-10.

Meanwhile, at Nakagusuku Wan, a suicide boat of the IJA 27th Suicide Boat Regiment successfully rammed cargo ship *Carina* (AK-74) at sunset, causing serious damage but only six wounded. *Carina* finished unloading her supplies and retired to Ulithi for repairs.

Most of *Kikisui* No. 5's 125 kamikazes (75 IJNAF and 50 IJAAF) began launching from Kyushu at 0500hrs, May 4, and were accompanied by 103 fighters. By then the Royal Navy's TF-57 had returned for its second *Iceberg* tour. Rawlings promptly launched dawn strikes against the Sakishimas' Miyako and Ishigaki airfields. Covered by their own CAP, battleships *King George V*, *Howe*, five cruisers, and six destroyers

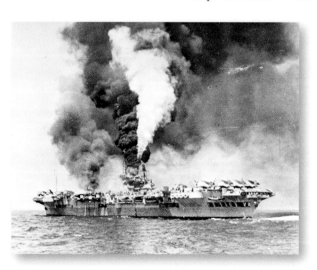

HMS *Formidable* shortly after being crashed by a Zero at 1131hrs, May 4. Much has been made about the durability of British armored flight decks compared with the American carriers. However, a close inspection of catastrophic episodes aboard US carriers suggests the British carriers' much lower casualty rates were a result of their much lower tempo of flight operations, which made runaway sympathetic detonations far less likely.
(© Imperial War Museum, A 29717)

detached from TF-57 at 1000hrs and shelled Japanese antiaircraft batteries at Nobara and Hirara airfields.

But at 1131hrs a Zero suddenly dove out of the overcast against *Formidable* and TF-57's weakened antiaircraft screen. After convoluted maneuvers by both attacker and target, the Zero finally crashed into *Formidable*'s flight deck, causing extensive damage, killing nine and wounding 47. Minutes later, a second Zero pancaked into *Indomitable* before sliding overboard and exploding harmlessly.

A diving Ki-61 Tony just misses escort carrier *Sangamon* at 1900hrs on the evening of May 4, 1945. Only a few radio antennae were damaged. But barely a half hour later, at 1933hrs, a twin-engined Ki-45 Nick fighter successfully slammed into *Sangamon* and exploded, causing severe fires and putting the carrier's survival in jeopardy. (Corbis via Getty Images)

Back at Okinawa's RPS-1, destroyers *Morrison* (DD-560) and *Ingraham* (DD-694), plus three escorting LCS craft (nicknamed "pallbearers" by the destroyermen) received the inevitable morning attack. *Ingraham* shot down six attackers before being crashed, losing 15 killed and 37 wounded. By 0825hrs *Morrison* had weathered four grazing hits or near-misses before taking two direct hits from crashing Zeros. Within five minutes she had received another two or three direct hits from crashing "Alf" biplanes, each carrying 1,000lb bombs, with the last detonating a 5in. magazine. *Morrison* sank ten minutes later, suffering 159 killed and 102 wounded; only 71 survived uninjured. Assisting *Morrison* survivors, *LSM(R)-190* was crashed at 0850hrs. She exploded and sank with 14 dead and 18 wounded. The three LCS escorts splashed nine attackers, with two LCSs surviving kamikaze crashes.

During an attack against RPS-12, a kamikaze crashed destroyer *Luce* (DD-522) at 0810hrs. Flooding rapidly, *Luce* slid under at 0815hrs before exploding violently underwater, taking 149 men with her. The same attack sank escorting *LSM(R)-190*, killing another 13 Americans.

At RPS-14, destroyer-minelayer *Shea* (DM-30) spotted a G4M Betty five miles distant; *Shea*'s vectored Corsair shot it down four minutes later at 0858hrs. This was apparently too late, as one minute later an *Ohka* came screaming into *Shea*'s superstructure at 475mph, killing 32 and wounding 91. *Shea* retired for repairs.

CAPs and antiaircraft fire had combined to repulse a Japanese attack against TF-51's Hagushi anchorage around 0830hrs, but ten minutes later a lone Ki-43 Oscar suddenly appeared. It dove on Deyo's TF-54 flagship, light cruiser *Birmingham*, then bombarding Naha airfield. The resulting crash killed 52 Americans, wounded 82, and relegated *Birmingham* to Pearl Harbor.

Formosa-based IJAAF planes attacked at twilight. At 1933hrs, a twin-engined Nick fighter simultaneously bombed and crashed escort carrier *Sangamon* (CVE-26) off Kerama Retto, triggering a gigantic explosion. Superb damage control saved the carrier, but 36 of her men were dead. *Sangamon* never returned to service.

Kikisui No. 5 had killed 589 Allied sailors on May 3–4, the worst two-day total of the campaign, and had sunk three destroyers and three LSM(R)s. Escort carrier *Sangamon*, light cruiser *Birmingham*, and several more destroyers were knocked out of the war. Privately, Nimitz masked his concern at the high casualties with the sardonic observation, "Anyway, we can produce new destroyers faster than they can build planes."

American morale lifted on May 8 when word arrived of Germany's unconditional surrender. Spruance celebrated by ordering all Fifth Fleet and Tenth Army guns to fire on enemy positions at noon. Tenth Army had by now decisively defeated the Japanese counteroffensive, killing 7,000 of Ushijima's men at a cost of just 700 US casualties. Ushijima's attempted nighttime counterlandings on both US flanks had been crushed by TF-51's alert "Flycatcher" patrols, backed by American troops ashore. As more sober IJA officers had predicted, counterattacking into American firepower had proved a disaster.

KIKISUI NO. 6, MAY 10–11

Off the Sakishimas, a kamikaze struck HMS *Formidable* on May 9, causing moderate damage that killed one and wounded eight. *Formidable* shortly resumed limited air operations. Back off Okinawa, kamikazes additionally crashed destroyer-escorts *Oberrender* (DE-344) and *England* (DE-635), knocking them out of the war and killing 45 Americans.

Kikisui No. 6 commenced the morning of May 10, comprising 150 kamikazes (80 IJAAF and 70 IJNAF) plus escorts. The brunt fell on RPS-15 off western Okinawa, where destroyers *Evans* (DD-552) and *Hugh W. Hadley* (DD-774) were attacked by an estimated 156 Japanese aircraft. Although horribly outnumbered, the Americans' Corsair CAP shot down 50 attackers before the Japanese got through at 0800hrs. Over the next 90 minutes the two violently maneuvering destroyers would claim a combined 42 kills before *Evans* was disabled by four kamikaze hits. Minutes later *Hugh W. Hadley* was knocked out by her third kamikaze hit. With his ship dead in the water and blazing uncontrollably, *Hugh W. Hadley*'s Commander Mullaney ordered all available colors hoisted: "If this ship is going down, she's going down with all flags flying." Escorting the destroyers were three LCS(L)s and one LSM(R), who themselves combined to splash 14 Japanese planes before the action mercifully ended. All six ships survived, but the destroyers were towed to Kerama Retto, having suffered a combined 60 killed and 94 wounded.

Commander Mullaney nevertheless praised his defending Corsairs: "When the [CAP] leader was asked to close and assist us, he replied, 'I am out of ammunition but I am sticking with you.' He then proceeded to fly his plane at enemy planes attacking in attempts to head them off. Towards the end of the battle I witnessed one Marine pilot attempting to ride off a suicide diving plane. This plane hit us but not vitally. I am willing to take my ship to the shores of Japan if I could have these Marines with me."

East of Okinawa, a G4M Betty bomber and four Ki-43 Oscars attacked RPS-5 at 0800hrs. One plane crashed destroyer-minelayer *Harry*

Seen from light carrier *Bataan*, Mitscher's flagship *Bunker Hill* billows smoke after being severely damaged by kamikazes. Mitscher himself had lost 13 staff members killed. His sea cabin and flag office aboard *Bunker Hill* had been destroyed by fire, including all of his clothes and most of his papers. At 1500hrs, Mitscher and 20 of his surviving staff began departing *Bunker Hill* for destroyer *English* (DD-696). (NHHC 80-G-274266)

F. Bauer (DM-26)'s stern, the kamikaze miraculously "plowing through the rack of depth charges and shoving them into the sea with none of them exploding." Escorting *LCS(L)-88* splashed two Oscars, the second scoring a posthumous 220lb bomb hit on her which killed nine and wounded seven.

May 11 found TG-58.3 and TG-58.4, including Mitscher's flagship *Bunker Hill*, 100nm east of Okinawa to provide direct air support and fighter cover to Tenth Army ashore. By now, TF-58 had been at sea for two months, and the unrelenting combat and flight operations had inevitably dulled American sailors' mental and physical acuity.

That morning the 721st Kokutai's Sub-Lieutenant Seizo Yasunori led six kamikazes out of Kanoya. By 1002hrs, Mitscher was informed of possible bogeys infiltrating the returning TF-58 strike to reach the US carriers. Two minutes later came an overhead Corsair's sudden frantic warning: *"Alert! Alert! Two planes diving on the Bunker Hill!"* Almost immediately, Yasunori's Zero dove out of low overcast toward *Bunker Hill* and released its payload. The 550lb bomb pierced the flight deck, exited the side of the hull, and exploded above water. Simultaneously, Yasunori's Zero caromed into the center of *Bunker Hill*'s flight deck, its gas tank exploding among 34 manned, armed, and fully fueled US fighters, before careening blazing over the side.

One minute later, Yasunori's wingman Ensign Kiyoshi Ogawa roared past *Bunker Hill*, climbed steeply into a roll, and then dove straight at the carrier. Ogawa released his 550lb bomb, which scored amidships and exploded in the gallery deck, slaughtering much of Mitscher's staff. Simultaneously, Ogawa deliberately slammed his Zero into *Bunker Hill*'s island just 100ft from Mitscher.

Mitscher's operations officer, Commander Jimmy Flatley, had just left the gallery deck when Ogawa's bomb struck, searing his back. Mitscher had observed the entire attack in silence, and just then emerged from the bridge to gaze at the blazing flight deck. The Flag Plot was choked with billowing smoke and Mitscher's chief-of-staff, a gasping, wheezing Commodore Arleigh Burke, ordered it evacuated. A third Zero then dove on *Bunker Hill*, but antiaircraft fire sent it blazing into the sea close aboard. Signaling *Essex*, Mitscher temporarily relinquished TF-58 command to TG-58.3's Sherman.

Aboard *Bunker Hill*, a cascade of gasoline explosions erupted from burning planes aft, while tracers sprayed haphazardly from detonating machine gun ammunition. Speed fell to 10kts and as the crew began intensive firefighting efforts, a slight list developed. Cruiser *Wilkes-Barre* and three destroyers came alongside to fight fires and rescue 300 men forced overboard. By 1130hrs damage was largely stabilized. Nevertheless, *Bunker Hill* had lost 393 men killed and 264 wounded in the deadliest kamikaze attack of the war. Most of *Bunker Hill*'s fighter pilots had been asphyxiated in their ready room. Mitscher would resume TF-58 command from *Enterprise* the following morning, but *Bunker Hill* never returned to service. The two-day

Seen from heavy cruiser *Wichita*, battleship *New Mexico* is crashed by a kamikaze at dusk, May 12. The attack killed 54 and wounded 19. After some anxious minutes, Fifth Fleet staff found Spruance manning a firehose. He calmly reminded his staff to check the kamikaze wreckage for codebooks. (NHHC 80-G-328653)

Kikisui No. 6 had killed over 463 Americans, making it the second-deadliest *Kikisui* of the campaign.

Kamikazes continued their assault on US flagships at sunset, May 12, when two kamikazes streaked in low towards Spruance's *New Mexico*. The battleship shot down one, but the second, a Ki-84 Frank, struck *New Mexico* amidships, igniting ready-service 20mm ammunition, and wrecking three boilers in the blast. *New Mexico* lost 54 killed and 119 wounded, with Spruance himself nearly a casualty. *New Mexico* nevertheless remained on station.

At dusk, May 13, a kamikaze slammed into destroyer *Bache* (DD-470), killing 41 and knocking her out of the war. Then at 1919hrs, a single Zero crashed destroyer-escort *Bright* (DE-747) while she was screening transports southwest of Okinawa. *Bright* was safely towed to Kerama Retto, suffering two wounded.

KYUSHU DIVERSION, MAY 13–14

Aboard *Enterprise*, Burke and Flatley repeatedly urged a reluctant Mitscher to hammer airfields on Kyushu. Mitscher believed more aircraft could be destroyed by remaining off Okinawa, and additionally reminded his subordinates that TF-58's priority was CAS to Tenth Army. Nevertheless, a dubious Mitscher relented and ordered TF-58's two front-line carrier Task Groups to close Kyushu the afternoon of May 12. After *Enterprise*'s night group heckled Kyushu airfields overnight, TG-58.1 and TG-58.3 launched the first daylight strikes against Kyushu air facilities on May 13, then hit Kyushu again on May 14.

At 0525hrs, May 14, some 28 Zeros, armed with 1,100lb bombs, sortied from Kanoya towards Mitscher's carriers cruising 130nm southeast of Kyushu. Forty fighters escorted them. Around 0645hrs *Enterprise* detected four incoming bogies. Three were shot down over TF-58, but the fourth, flown by Sub-Lieutenant Shunsuke Tomiyasu, continued closing. Using clouds for cover, Tomiyasu approached *Enterprise* from astern. Already struck by TF-58 flak, at 0657hrs Tomiyasu's blazing Zero suddenly appeared 200ft above *Enterprise*, which erupted with antiaircraft fire. Although seeming to have overflown his target, Tomiyasu suddenly snap-rolled his burning Zero onto its back and dove almost vertically into *Enterprise*'s flight deck.

Observing from *Enterprise*'s exposed bridge wing, Flatley rushed back inside and shouted to take cover just as Tomiyasu's kamikaze hit. The thunderous explosion blew *Enterprise*'s forward elevator 400ft in the air, rattled the carrier's bridge, and flung shrapnel against her island. As Flatley emerged from cover he observed an unsmiling Mitscher, arms crossed, standing amid the smoking wreckage. "Jimmy," Mitscher growled, "tell my Task Group commanders that if the Japs keep this up they're going to grow hair on my head yet."

Veteran fast carrier *Enterprise* is crashed by Sub-Lieutenant Shunsuke Tomiyasu's Zero off Kyushu, May 14, 1945. *Enterprise*'s forward elevator has been blown hundreds of feet in the air. *Enterprise* remains arguably the most beloved and battle-proven warship in US Navy history, but her combat career ended here off Kyushu. (NHHC 80-G-323565)

Enterprise remained on station, but her flight deck was out of action. TF-58 splashed three more planes before Japanese attacks ended at 0800hrs. That evening TF-58 retired from Kyushu. The following morning, May 15, Mitscher transferred to carrier *Randolph*, his third flagship in five days. *Enterprise* would detach for repairs in the United States on May 16, having lost 14 dead and 68 wounded. Her war too was over.

During May 13–14, TF-58 had flown 700 daylight strike sorties and claimed 72 Japanese planes shot down, plus 240 destroyed or damaged on the ground. TF-58 aerial losses had been 14 planes and 17 aircrew. Nevertheless, after reflecting on his and Burke's ill-advised Kyushu attack, Flatley decided Mitscher had been right, conceding, "Mitscher never made a tactical error in the employment of the Task Force and its aircraft."

AIR AND NAVAL GUNFIRE SUPPORT OF TENTH ARMY

Each day from Turner's flagship *Eldorado*, Captain Dick Whitehead (USN), Commander Air Support Control Units (CASCU), had allocated land- and air-based planes their assigned missions; Whitehead had already directed 6,908 CAS missions through early April. Additionally, once Colonel Vernon Megee's USMC control units were established ashore, they coordinated an additional 10,506 CAS sorties which would deliver 4,725 tons of bombs, 1,116 tanks of napalm, and 37,653 5in. rockets against Japanese positions. Megee had initially refused to work through Whitehead upon going ashore, instead reporting to Buckner. Upon hearing this, Nimitz informed Turner: "Tell Megee to report to Whitehead or return to Pearl Harbor." Megee chose the former. Meanwhile, Whitehead, due for promotion, was relieved as CASCU on April 18 by Rear Admiral Mel Pride.

On April 13, battleships *Texas* and *West Virginia*, four cruisers, and six destroyers opened a three-day pre-landing bombardment against volcanic Ie Shima, five miles off northwestern Okinawa. Early on April 16, Rear Admiral Reifsnider's Ie Shima Attack Group (TG-51.21) landed the US 77th Division to seize Ie Shima's valuable airfield. After five days of bitter fighting against well-entrenched Japanese, the Americans declared the isle secure, having lost 172 troops killed and 902 wounded. By May 10 Ie Shima was hosting P-47N Thunderbolts of the 318th Fighter Group. Within four days the P-47s were flying radar picket CAPs. The 318th was shortly joined by P-47s of the 507th and 413th Fighter Groups; all would fly Okinawa CAS missions throughout May.

On May 11, Tenth Army had begun a major offensive against Ushijima's inner Shuri defenses. A few days later came Okinawa's torrential summer rains, which continued for weeks. Although *Iceberg* remained unfinished, Spruance and Turner needed to rest and plan for Operation *Olympic*, the scheduled November 1945 invasion of Kyushu. Fifth Fleet and TF-51 would accordingly be relinquished

A Marine FG Corsair attacks an Okinawa target with rockets. Ironically, the carrier aviators (both Navy and USMC) were more experienced in CAS tactics than TAF personnel, meaning *Iceberg*'s air defense typically devolved onto TAF. By late April, TAF had flown 3,521 CAP sorties and claimed 143 enemy kills, a TAF officer recalling, "It seemed strange for planes off the carriers to come in for close support missions, passing Marine planes flying out for CAP duty." (NHHC USMC 129356)

to Admiral Bill Halsey and newly promoted Vice Admiral Harry Hill. On May 17, Hill formally relieved Turner as commander of TF-51 and began answering directly to Buckner.

Meanwhile, US naval gunfire support was proving relentless. To provide direct fire support, Turner had permanently assigned two gunships to each Tenth Army regiment, including at least one destroyer to provide night illumination. Turner additionally assigned one or two battleships or cruisers to each divisional and corps headquarters; these ships furnished deep interdiction fire. TF-54 gunfire support would ultimately expend 23,210 12in. and 14in. rounds, 31,550 8in. HC rounds, 45,450 6in. HC rounds, and over 184,000 5in. rounds through June 21.

According to the official US Army history:

> The continuous presence of the tremendous fleet, aligned on the enemy's flanks, provided the ground forces with the constant support of its great mobile batteries, capable of hurling a vast weight of metal from a variety of weapons ranging from rockets to 16-inch rifles. Naval gunfire was employed longer and in greater quantities in the battle of Okinawa than in any other in history. It supported the ground troops and complemented the artillery from the day of the landing until action moved to the extreme southern tip of the island, where the combat area was so restricted there was a danger of hitting American troops.

Destroyer *Isherwood* (DD-520) bombards Ie Shima, mid-April 1945. *Isherwood's* gunfire is either preparing the 77th Division's landing or already supporting the division ashore. Ie Shima proved more heavily defended than expected, but its airfield would prove a major asset once captured and repaired. Ie Shima's distinctive 565ft Mount Gusuku is visible in the background. (NHHC 80-G-K-4732)

Battleship *Mississippi*, assigned to destroy Shuri Castle, delivered 1,600 tons of 14in. shells in six weeks of action. Her companion, battleship *Colorado*, would deliver 2,060 tons of 16in. shells through May 21. Major-General Pedro Del Valle, whose 1st Marine Division was engaged in the reduction of Shuri, reported to *Colorado*: "Your superb shooting has been a constant inspiration to our troops … every Jap captured reveals the awe and fear with which all Japs regard your gunfire."

Shore bombardment nevertheless remained dangerous. At 0719hrs, May 18, destroyer *Longshaw* (DD-559) ran aground while preparing to fire on Naha airfield. Attempts to tow *Longshaw* repeatedly failed, and at 1100hrs Japanese coastal battery fire began straddling her. *Longshaw* retaliated before being rapidly struck several times, triggering a catastrophic magazine explosion that annihilated the forward half of the ship. *Longshaw's* mortally wounded skipper ordered the destroyer abandoned. Of *Longshaw's* 291 men, 86 were killed and 97 wounded.

However, the battle's turning point suddenly emerged at midday May 26, when a *New York* spotter plane observed a large formation of Japanese troops and trucks jamming roads south of Shuri in apparent retreat. Almost immediately, heavy cruiser *New Orleans* kicked off a deafening fleet-wide naval bombardment against the exposed concentration of 4,000 Japanese troops and their vulnerable heavy equipment. Within minutes, 50 scrambling TAF Corsairs would brave the naval shelling to help strafe and bomb the fleeing Japanese, a USMC history describing the slaughter as "a field day." Del Valle observed approvingly that the "Nips were caught on [the] road with kimonos down." That night, US naval guns unleashed harassment and interdiction fire against roads and junctions leading south from Shuri.

Tenth Army penetrated the now nearly deserted Naha on May 25, fully occupying it five days later. The Americans also captured Shuri Castle on May 29 and all Shuri on May 31. Since mid-April, the vast majority of Ushijima's 32nd Army, over 60,000 troops, had been killed tenaciously defending the fortified Shuri line. Shuri's conquest signaled the beginning of the end of the battle for Okinawa.

Stranded destroyer *Longshaw* (DD-559) explodes from a catastrophic magazine detonation, May 18, 1945. *Longshaw* had just been hit by Japanese coastal artillery fire off Naha, after having been immobilized all morning since running aground several hours earlier. The view is from light cruiser *Vincennes*. (NHHC 80-G-343583)

KIKISUI NO. 7, MAY 23–25

At dusk, May 17, Japanese planes had attacked the six-ship RPS-9 southwest of Kerama Retto, resulting in ten dead when a Ki-44 Tojo crashed destroyer *Douglas H. Fox* (DD-779). The following night, a low-flying kamikaze hit *LST-808* off Ie Shima, killing 17. Two days later, kamikazes damaged destroyer *Thatcher* (DD-514), destroyer-escort *John C. Butler* (DE-339), and destroyer-transports *Chase* (APD-54) and *Register* (APD-92), while a horizontal bomber damaged destroyer-transport *Tattnall* (APD-19), killing a combined 14 Americans.

The three-night *Kikisui* No. 7 began after dark on May 23, and ultimately totaled 165 kamikazes (100 IJAAF and 65 IJNAF). Its first 24 hours were unimpressive, with TF-58 hitting Kyushu airfields at dawn, May 24, and only *LCS(L)-121* suffering light bomb damage. Nevertheless, late that evening, heavy Japanese nighttime raids bombed US airfields at Kadena, Yontan, and Ie Shima.

Such actions, however, proved mere diversions for the unfolding Operation *Giretsu*. Around midnight, Yontan airfield lookouts spotted five Sixth Air Army Ki-21 Sally bombers approaching overhead. US gunners destroyed four, but the surviving Sally successfully crash-landed in a nighttime spray of flames and sparks before disgorging ten heavily armed IJA commandos. They immediately began lobbing grenades and incendiaries at parked US planes. Sowing wild nocturnal mayhem, the Japanese killed two Americans and wounded 18, destroyed nine US aircraft, damaged 29 more, and set a fuel dump ablaze, destroying 70,000gals of avgas. After 12 hours of chaos, US troops hunted the commandos down and exterminated them to a man. *Giretsu*'s partial success was achieved despite US fighters and antiaircraft fire (both ground and naval) claiming 150 total Japanese planes on May 24.

Shortly after 0800hrs, May 25, kamikazes crashed minesweeper *Spectacle* (AM-305), inspiring her abandonment. *LSM-135* began rescuing *Spectacle* survivors before also being crashed. She was beached on a reef and abandoned. *Spectacle* however was partially re-manned and towed to

A wrecked IJAAF Ki-21 Sally at Yontan following the May 23/24 *Giretsu* air commando raid. US authorities counted 60 Japanese bodies, mostly from the five Sally bombers shot down. The Japanese air commando raid was creative, but never came close to turning the tide of battle. (WW2DB)

A Marine L-5 observation plane flies over a devastated Naha, May 1945. The four Marine Observation (VMO) squadrons flew 3,486 sorties, undertaking artillery spotting, photoreconnaissance, and medical evacuation missions. A USMC artillery officer called the L-5s "the unsung heroes of Marine aviation ... often they would fly past cave openings at the same level so they could look in and see if a gun [was] there." (Corbis via Getty Images)

safety. An hour later at 0905hrs a kamikaze struck destroyer *Stormes* (DD-780), which withdrew to Kerama Retto. Then at 1125hrs, two kamikazes hit destroyer-transport *Bates* (APD-47) just off Ie Shima. The abandoned, burning *Bates* was towed to Ie Shima, where she capsized. Kamikazes additionally crashed and damaged destroyer *Guest* (DD-472), destroyer-minesweeper *Butler* (DMS-29), destroyer-transport *Roper* (APD-20), and destroyer *Barry* (DD-248) 35nm northwest of Okinawa, setting her ablaze. *Barry* was towed to Kerama Retto and decommissioned. Finally, an unidentified Japanese plane torpedoed Liberty ship *William R. Allison*. The following day, May 26, kamikazes crashed destroyer-escort *O'Neill* (DE-188), destroyer-minesweeper *Forrest* (DMS-24), and subchaser *PC-1603*. In all, the May 23–26 raids killed 103 US sailors.

Believing the fast carriers' continued value off Okinawa had become dubious, back on May 18 Mitscher had requested that TF-58 be relieved from its Okinawa station. Spruance regretfully declined. A week later an increasingly weary Mitscher reported: "For two and a half months [Task Force 58] operated daily in a 60nm square area East of Okinawa, less than 350nm from Kyushu. This was necessitated by the restricted area available and the necessity for being able to cover [the] Amami Gunto airfields, intercept air raids before they could reach Okinawa, and still furnish air support to ground forces. There was no other location from which all these things could be done."

Reflecting on the months of unrelenting stress, tedium, and fatigue, TG-58.1's screen commander, Captain Tom Hederman, signaled Rear Admiral J.J. Jocko Clark: "See Hebrews 13, verse 8." Consulting his Bible aboard *Hornet*, Clark read: *"Jesus Christ the same yesterday, and today, and forever."* Amused, Clark forwarded the verse to his entire Task Group, adding, "No disrespect intended." Clark then signaled Mitscher, "What the hell are we doing out here, anyway?" Mitscher's response: "We are a high-speed stationary target for the Japanese air force." Indeed, TF-58 had already suffered over 2,000 *Iceberg* fatalities.

Iceberg's relentless operations had also taken its toll on Rawlings' TF-57. *Formidable*, severely damaged by a hangar fire, withdrew for Sydney on May 22. Now down to three battered carriers, TF-57 launched its last strikes and retired from the Okinawa area late on May 25, having fulfilled the Royal Navy's *Iceberg* mission. Rawlings would receive the following message from Spruance on May 27: "On completion of your two months' operations as a Task Force of the Fifth Fleet in support of the capture of Okinawa, I wish to express to you and to the officers and men under your command, my appreciation of the fine work you have done and the splendid spirit of co-operation in which you have done it. To the American portion of the Fifth Fleet, Task Force 57 has typified the great traditions of the Royal Navy. Signed Spruance."

TF-57 carriers had flown 4,893 *Iceberg* sorties, including 2,073 strike sorties that expended 958 tons of bombs and 950 3in. rockets. Some 160 planes had been lost, including 72 operational casualties (of which 61 were Seafire landing accidents). Kamikaze hits had destroyed 32 planes, while *Formidable*'s hangar fire had claimed 30 more. Just 26 aircraft had been lost in combat. TF-57 had suffered 126 total casualties. These included 85 men killed or missing, of whom 41 were aviators.

KIKISUI NO. 8, MAY 27–29

Admiral Bill Halsey's new flagship, battleship *Missouri*, anchored off the western coast of Okinawa on May 26. Halsey conferred with Spruance and his staff aboard *Missouri* that morning, then went ashore to confer with Buckner in the afternoon. Over 90 US ships had been sunk or heavily damaged off Okinawa since mid-March. Halsey described the situation in his autobiography:

> Once again the fleet was being held in static defense instead of being sent to hit the enemy where it hurt. This strategy was worse than unprofitable, it was expensive ... Kamikazes had been attacking the Fleet ferociously. Our picket ships—destroyers and destroyer escorts—were being smashed almost daily. We had given the enemy the initiative, instead of blanketing his home fields and burning every plane we could find ... [I asked] Ray Spruance how well the SOWESPAC air force, based in the Philippines, was neutralizing Formosa. He said bitterly, "They've destroyed a great many sugar mills, railroad trains, and other equipment." I blew up. "Sugar mills can't damage our fleet! Why the hell don't they destroy their *planes*?"
>
> The immobilization of the fleet could be based on two facts: first, the Japs' stubborn defense, which had prevented our ground forces from obtaining airfields where they could base enough planes for their own protection; second, the ground forces' failure to install enough radars to permit the withdrawal of our patrols and pickets. As a result, Ray had had to continue his support, despite the dangerous exposure of the fleet and the fact that his ships were long overdue for repair and his men for rest.

Halsey confronted Buckner, who had been unaware of the radar construction issue but insisted it would get fixed. "I will always maintain," Halsey recalled, "that if you want something done quickly, a five-minute conversation is infinitely better than a five-thousand-word report in triplicate."

Late that evening, *Missouri* departed Okinawa for the fast carriers, Halsey relating, "As the *Missouri* stood out, I gave orders for her to drop some 16-inch calling cards on the enemy's doorstep; I wanted him to know I was back." A few hours later, at midnight May 27, Fleet command officially passed from Spruance to Halsey. Fifth Fleet became Third Fleet, while Hill's TF-51 became TF-31. As morning broke *Missouri* rendezvoused with the fast carriers. Vice Admiral John McCain then broke his flag aboard carrier *Shangri-La*, assuming fast carrier command and sending the well-worn

Vice Admiral Bill Halsey (left) confers with Vice Admiral Raymond Spruance (right) aboard battleship *New Mexico*, May 27, 1945. Halsey, a New Jersey native, was unable to return to his favorite flagship, as battleship *New Jersey* was back in Puget Sound being overhauled. Instead, Halsey broke his flag in *New Jersey*'s younger sister *Missouri*, dispatched to Guam to pick Halsey up. (Navsource)

Mitscher home. TF-58 accordingly became TF-38. Yet relief for the fast carriers' remaining personnel remained elusive, TG-38.3's Rear Admiral Ted Sherman admitting, "Everyone is dead tired; we have been out of Ulithi 76 days now."

Halsey was immediately faced with *Kikisui* No. 8, totaling 110 kamikazes. On May 27 alone, kamikazes crashed and damaged destroyers *Braine* (DD-530) and *Anthony* (DD-518), destroyer-minesweeper *Southard* (DMS-10), destroyer-transports *Loy* (APD-56) and *Rednour* (APD-102), surveying ship *Dutton* (AGS-8), subchaser *PCS-1396*, and degaussing vessel *YDG-10*. Additionally, a *Kaiten* from Japanese submarine *I-367* struck destroyer-escort *Gilligan* (DE-508) but failed to explode.

The following morning, May 28, several kamikazes attacked destroyers *Drexler* (DD-741) and *Lowry* (DD-770). Four were shot down, but two crashed *Drexler*, triggering a tremendous explosion. *Drexler* rolled over and sank in less than 60 seconds, taking 164 Americans with her. Barely thirty minutes later, at 0730hrs, a kamikaze struck transport *Sandoval* (APA-194) in Nakagusuku Wan. Kamikazes additionally crashed civilian US freighters *Mary A. Livermore*, *Josiah Snelling*, and *Brown Victory* off Okinawa, killing seven USN personnel and eight merchant mariners. Finally, shortly before midnight, a bomb-laden Zero crashed *LCS(L)-119*, causing a raging fire that killed ten and seriously wounded 18. The next day, kamikazes damaged destroyer *Shubrick* (DD-639) and destroyer-transport *Tatum* (APD-81). The May 27–29 *Kikisui* No. 8 had claimed one destroyer sunk, several destroyers and merchantmen damaged, and over 250 Americans killed.

Two days later, escort carrier *Anzio* (CVE-57) detected *I-361* some 400nm southeast of Okinawa. *I-361* dove underwater but was nevertheless obliterated beneath a barrage of sonobuoys, 5in. rockets, and a Mark 24 "Fido" acoustic homing torpedo dropped by *Anzio* Avengers.

OKINAWA SECURED, JUNE–JULY 1945

Clark's TG-38.1 attacked Okinawa on June 2–3, while Radford's TG-38.4 attacked Kyushu with fighter sweeps. Poor situational awareness by Halsey and McCain then saw Third Fleet stumble into a typhoon the early morning of June 5. Clark's TG-38.1 and Beary's TG-30.8 received the worst; they reported 110–120kt wind gusts and 100ft seas before Third Fleet fully escaped the retroactively named "Typhoon Viper."

Clark's fast carriers *Hornet* and *Bennington* had each lost their forward 25ft of flight deck, while carriers *Belleau Wood* and *San Jacinto*, heavy cruiser *Baltimore*, light cruiser *Duluth*, and destroyer *Samuel N. Moore* were also damaged. Most spectacularly, high seas had ripped off 104ft of heavy cruiser *Pittsburgh*'s bow. Superb seamanship allowed *Pittsburgh* to limp to Guam. Beary's escort carriers *Windham Bay* (CVE-92) and

Salamaua (CVE-96) suffered wrecked flight decks, while tanker *Millicoma* (AO-73) was heavily damaged. In all, Third Fleet suffered six killed, while 76 planes were destroyed.

The aggressive Clark nevertheless insisted his battered carriers maintain offensive flight operations. However, at 1414hrs, June 6, turbulence from *Hornet*'s collapsed forward flight deck caused a fighter to crash on take-off. Undeterred, Clark had *Hornet* launch her next 24-fighter sweep over the stern while steaming 18kts in reverse.

Meanwhile, *Kikisui* No. 9 had commenced on June 3, its measly 50 kamikazes heavily stymied by Typhoon Viper. Nevertheless, kamikazes immediately damaged *LCI(L)-90* and cargo ship *Allegan* (AK-225). Two days later, on June 5, a kamikaze crashed battleship *Mississippi*, killing her chaplain and wounding 11, but causing little damage. Two miles away and just two minutes later, heavy cruiser *Louisville* opened fire on a Ki-61 Tony streaking in at low altitude. The blazing Tony nevertheless crashed *Louisville* amidships, causing widespread but uncritical damage that killed eight and wounded 46.

On June 6, destroyer-minelayers *J. William Ditter* (DM-31) and *Harry F. Bauer* (DM-26) fell under kamikaze attack. They shot down several before *J. William Ditter* was crashed, with *Harry F. Bauer* apparently left unharmed. Since L-Day the impossibly charmed *Harry F. Bauer* had already shot down 13 attackers, weathered a dud torpedo, and shrugged off a direct kamikaze hit that slid harmlessly overboard. Now, unknown to her crew, she would spend the next 17 days carrying around a live 550lb bomb before it was discovered.

The following morning, June 7, a Zero strafed and then crashed escort carrier *Natoma Bay* (CVE-62), killing one and wounding four, while destroyer *Anthony* (DD-515) was holed by a kamikaze near-miss but suffered no losses. As *Kikisui* No. 9 fizzled out on June 7, Ugaki's Fifth Air Fleet admitted, "It is believed that the operation in Okinawa is in its final phase … Despite the efforts of the Army, Navy, and Air Force in carrying out *Ten-Go*, satisfactory results were not obtained." Adding insult to injury, the following day TG-38.1 and TG-38.4 launched 200 fighters against southern Kyushu airfields.

On June 10, a Val dove on radar picket destroyer *William D. Porter* (DD-579) 40 miles northwest of Okinawa. Evasive maneuvering caused the kamikaze to plunge under *William D. Porter*'s keel before it exploded, lifting the destroyer out of the water. *William D. Porter* ultimately sank without loss. That same day TG-38.1 bombed and shelled Minami Daito island, including Rear Admiral Jack Shafroth's three fast battleships *Alabama*, *Indiana*, and *Massachusetts*. That afternoon TF-38 concluded *Iceberg* operations and retired for Leyte-Samar after 89 straight days off Okinawa.

Heavy cruiser *Pittsburgh* steams for Guam, her bow having been wrenched off during Typhoon Viper early on June 5, 1945. Just 15 minutes before the catastrophic failure, *Pittsburgh*'s Captain John Gingrich had dogged all watertight bulkheads, and ordered Battle Stations, evacuating *Pittsburgh*'s forward berthing compartments, saving scores of men. *Pittsburgh*'s errant bow was discovered and towed to Guam. US sailors jokingly referred to the bow as USS *McKeesport* (a suburb of Pittsburgh). (Navsource)

Destroyer *William D. Porter* (DD-579) slowly capsizes and sinks on June 10, 1945. In November 1943 *William D. Porter* had accidentally fired a torpedo at battleship *Iowa*, carrying President Roosevelt and the entire Joint Chiefs of Staff. *Iowa* evaded the torpedo after the destroyer sheepishly alerted the battleship. Although the entire crew was arrested, Roosevelt insisted no one be punished. But at Okinawa *William D. Porter*'s luck finally ran out. (WW2DB)

By June 12, the IJAAF's entire operational strength stood at just 50 fighters and 50 kamikazes. Similarly, IJN staff admitted, "The strength of our Naval Air Force which is expected to attack the enemy anchorage at Okinawa has been reduced to almost nothing." Nevertheless, at 2030hrs, June 16, destroyer *Twiggs* (DD-591) was hit "first by a torpedo and then by the plane that dropped it." The blazing, exploding *Twiggs* sank an hour later, suffering 152 dead, including her skipper.

By June 18, Tenth Army had begun its final push to eradicate Japanese resistance on Okinawa. *Ten-Go*'s final gasp, the two-day *Kikisui* No. 10, commenced June 21 and totaled just 45 kamikazes. That evening, kamikazes penetrated Kerama Retto and crashed seaplane tenders *Curtiss* (AV-4) and *Kenneth Whiting* (AV-14), knocking *Curtiss* out of the war with 41 killed and 28 wounded. *LSM-59* was towing destroyer *Barry*'s hulk when kamikazes sank them both; *LSM-59* suffered two dead and eight wounded. Then, when destroyer-escort *Halloran* (DE-305) shot down a kamikaze at point-blank range, its bomb detonated, killing three men. The following day, a kamikaze seriously damaged *LST-534*.

However, by now IJA 32nd Army transmissions had fallen silent, forcing a bitterly regretful Ugaki to conclude the worst. Brooding to his diary, Ugaki felt "greatly responsible for the calamity" yet admitted there seemed no alternative course that might have brought success.

Tenth Army had in fact completed its conquest of Okinawa late on June 21, when the US 7th Division wiped out the last cornered pocket of Japanese resistance on a lonely hilltop above the sea. Hours later Lieutenant-General Ushijima committed suicide. Shockingly preceding him in death was his adversary, Lieutenant-General Simon Buckner, whom a Japanese shell had killed on June 18. In honor of the fallen general, the Americans renamed Okinawa's Nakagusuku Wan as Buckner Bay. Major-General Roy Geiger (USMC) replaced Buckner as Tenth Army commander, but by dawn June 22 the land battle of Okinawa was essentially over. US authorities declared Okinawa officially secure on July 2.

Allied forces had suffered 49,246 total casualties during *Iceberg*, including 12,605 killed. Of these, 7,613 belonged to Tenth Army, while naval fatalities reached 4,992 (4,907 USN and 85 Royal Navy). *Iceberg* naval losses totaled 36 ships sunk and 374 damaged (including six British ships damaged). The Americans officially counted 107,539 Japanese military dead on Okinawa, with 7,455 Japanese captured. Combined with 42,000 civilian deaths, over 20,000 Japanese troops buried by bombardments, and perhaps 10,000 killed in the air and at sea, total Japanese and Okinawan fatalities surpassed 180,000.

A USMC history declared Okinawa "the culmination of amphibious development in the Pacific War." By *Iceberg*'s conclusion "more ships were used, more troops put ashore, more supplies transported, more bombs dropped, [and] more naval guns fired against shore targets" than in any previous battle. Fifth/Third Fleet had additionally landed some 557,000 tons of supplies over the Hagushi beaches in support of Tenth Army.

The last photograph ever taken of Lieutenant-General Simon Buckner, just moments before he was killed by shrapnel from an exploding Japanese artillery shell on June 18, 1945. Buckner was the highest-ranking US officer to die in Pacific War combat. (USMC)

Similarly, USMC air controller Colonel Vernon Megee deemed *Iceberg* "the culmination of air support doctrine in the Pacific." Between April 1 and June 21, TAF and carrier planes had flown a combined 14,244 CAS sorties, with over 60 percent by US escort carriers. TAF fighters had mounted over 29,000 total sorties, mostly in the air defense role. Its pilots would ultimately claim 625 air-to-air kills. Additionally, Durgin's escort carriers had flown 18,133 *Iceberg* sorties, expended nearly 2,000 tons of bombs and 30,000 rockets, and claimed 280 enemy planes, while losing 65 aircraft (32 operationally). Geiger later reported that US air support had been "outstanding and contributed materially to a speedy and successful completion of the campaign."

Between April 1 and June 30, 1945, Allied forces had lost 763 planes in the Okinawa campaign, including 305 operationally. Of 458 combat losses, 74 were to enemy aircraft and 384 to antiaircraft fire. US carriers had lost 565 aircraft to all causes. The marines had lost 64 planes and the British 98, not including those destroyed aboard damaged carriers. The balance of lost aircraft consisted of B-29s and USN patrol planes.

An FG Corsair rockets Japanese positions at Okinawa, June 1945. Each Corsair could carry eight high-velocity 5in. "Holy Moses" rockets, or 2,000lb of bombs. Ironically, US close air support at Okinawa was mostly provided by carrier planes rather than the Okinawa-based TAF, but in general American CAS proved extremely effective. (NHHC 127-GW-520-126420)

Full IJAAF statistics are unknown, but the IJNAF flew 3,700 sorties during the Okinawa campaign. Combined with 605 known IJAAF *tokko* attacks and additional IJAAF conventional attacks, total Japanese sorties in defense of Okinawa probably reached 6,000. Of these, at least 1,900 were kamikazes, including 1,465 during the ten *Kikisui* operations. Combined IJAAF/IJNAF combat losses during *Iceberg* exceeded 4,000 aircraft.

As a major and obvious staging base for Operation *Olympic*, Okinawa remained under intermittent Japanese aerial and naval attacks until war's end. Early on July 24, the *Kaiten*-armed submarine *I-53* ambushed US convoy TU-99.1.18, which had recently departed Buckner Bay for the Philippines. After depth-charging a *Kaiten* to the surface, destroyer-escort *Underhill* (DE-682) promptly rammed it and fatally exploded, taking 112 of her 234 American crewmen with her.

Back off Okinawa, destroyer *Callaghan* (DD-792) had shot down 12 kamikazes during *Iceberg*, but shortly after midnight, July 30, she was done in by a K5Y "Willow" biplane, whose wood-and-fabric airframe foiled *Callaghan*'s proximity-fuzed antiaircraft shells. *Callaghan* lost 47 men and proved the last US ship sunk by kamikaze in World War II. The following night, the Willows attacked again, crashing destroyer *Cassin Young* (DD-793) and killing 22 aboard. Finally, on August 12 a single Japanese plane would penetrate Buckner Bay before torpedoing and nearly sinking battleship *Pennsylvania*, killing another 20 Americans.

The battle for Okinawa had been brutal and hard-fought, producing 17 percent of all USN/USMC losses in the Pacific War. Unsurprisingly, Winston Churchill eulogized *Iceberg* best: "The strength of willpower, devotion and technical resources applied by the United States to this task, joined with the death struggle of the enemy ... places this battle among the most intense and famous of military history."

AFTERMATH

Iwo Jima's ultimate utility proved highly questionable. Iwo proved too remote to make an effective fighter base, yet was too small to stage anything else. Iwo Jima mounted only ten dedicated fighter escort missions, compared to 147 major B-29 missions launched against Japan between March and August 1945. Indeed, after his March 1945 switch to night tactics, LeMay would claim, "I was much more worried about B-29s shooting each other than I was about any ... ill-equipped and inexperienced Japanese night fighters."

Some 2,251 B-29s and 24,761 aircrew did make landings at Iwo Jima by war's end. However, almost all were for routine refuelings or for training missions, not combat damage. Countless B-29s landed at Iwo several times, and of those crewmen who did crash at sea, 50 percent were rescued. The widely celebrated claim that more aircrew were saved by Iwo Jima than marines killed is therefore suspect. More importantly, it must be noted that securing Iwo Jima as an emergency B-29 landing field had never been anyone's objective, and only afterwards was seized by US officers and American journalists as a desperate fig leaf to justify *Detachment*'s unexpectedly staggering cost.

By July 1945, some 245,000 US troops were ashore at Okinawa and outlying islands, including 87,000 US construction troops building 25 major airfields. The USN's huge new facilities, gearing up to mount Operation *Olympic*, would eventually cover 31 square miles. Meanwhile, the first Okinawa-based B-29s raided the Home Islands the night of August 14/15. Japan surrendered the following morning. In the end, no invasion was ever staged from Okinawa.

Although Japan flew three times as many kamikazes against the Allies at Okinawa as at the Philippines, the rate of hits and near-misses plunged from 26.8 percent at the Philippines to 14.8 percent at Okinawa. After June and October 1944, April 1945 proved the IJNAF's third-costliest month of the war, with 1,510 aircrew killed. Aerial attacks nevertheless sank escort carrier *Bismarck Sea*, and knocked fast carriers *Saratoga*, *Franklin*, *Illustrious*, *Intrepid*, *Bunker Hill*, and *Enterprise* out of the war, plus escort carrier *Sangamon* and battleships *Maryland*, *Mississippi*, and *Pennsylvania*. Yet, off Okinawa, the flimsy kamikazes ultimately sank no warship larger than a destroyer, nor did kamikazes ever sink an armored warship. Despite its horrifying nature, the kamikaze failed as a psychological weapon. Japanese suicide attacks proved unable to break Allied morale at the front, nor did they cause national resolve to waver at home.

Allied individuals and small units proved consistently flexible and innovative in combat. However, US flag officers largely clung to their original *Detachment* and *Iceberg* plans to their bitter, drawn-out ends, displaying little operational imagination once underway. US leadership paid for reduced American risk by implicitly accepting increased American casualties. However, at both Iwo Jima and Okinawa the dubious tradeoff ultimately succeeded; Japanese inventiveness and tenacity inevitably succumbed to the Americans' overwhelming organization and firepower.

THE WARSHIPS TODAY

Many US warships that fought off Iwo Jima and Okinawa have been preserved as museums in the United States. Several are kamikaze survivors from the Okinawa campaign, including battleship *Missouri* at Pearl Harbor, battleship *Texas* in her namesake state, and destroyer *Laffey*, at Charleston, South Carolina, where she is kept alongside a fellow East China Sea veteran, fast carrier *Yorktown*. Another preserved kamikaze survivor is destroyer *Kidd* at Baton Rouge, Louisiana. *Kidd* is the world's last destroyer surviving in World War II configuration.

On August 1, 1985, the Japanese-crewed submersible *Pisces II* positively identified the wreck of *Yamato*. She lies in two major pieces at a depth of 1,410ft, surrounded by a large debris field. Expeditions in 1999 and 2016 recorded video footage and recovered some small artifacts, including eating utensils and a bugle. Traditional accounts of the *Yamato* battle (including this one) conservatively acknowledge only 9–12 confirmed torpedo hits on *Yamato*. This number is based heavily on credible eyewitness accounts from *Yamato*'s few survivors, and dismisses most American claims as exaggerations. However, recent forensic analysis of the wreck suggests *Yamato* may have absorbed at least 16 and possibly as many as 22 torpedoes during her final battle, including up to nine torpedoes on her starboard side and six in her exposed starboard keel. If true, such staggering punishment exceeds even *Musashi*'s ordeal as the heaviest bombardment ever endured in naval history.

USMC Colonel R.P. Ross defies Japanese rifle fire to raise the US flag over Okinawa's Shuri Castle, May 29, 1945. Japan surrendered less than three months later, making Okinawa the last major amphibious operation of World War II. (Wikimedia)

FURTHER READING

Literature specifically devoted to the full spectrum of Iwo Jima and Okinawa air–sea combat remains scarce. However, official and semi-official US government histories make excellent starting points and include the US Army's *The Last Battle* and *Reports of General MacArthur (Vol. II Part II)*; the USAF's *The Pacific: Matterhorn to Nagasaki*; the USN's *The Official Chronology of the U.S. Navy in World War II* and *The Amphibians Came to Conquer (Vol. II)*; Samuel E. Morison's semi-official (USN) *Victory in the Pacific 1945*; the USMC's *History of Marine Corps Operations in World War II: Western Pacific Operations*; and USMC monographs *Iwo Jima: Amphibious Epic* and *Okinawa: Victory in the Pacific*. Additionally, TF-51 and

TF-58 produced excellent Iwo Jima and Okinawa post-action reports, while the USN's many online "H-Grams" are also well detailed.

Illuminating Japanese primary sources include *Japanese Monograph JM-86: War History of the 5th Air Fleet From 10 February 1945 to 19 August 1945*; Tameichi Hara's memoirs *Japanese Destroyer Captain*; Mitsuru Yoshida's first-person account *Requiem for Battleship Yamato*; and Admiral Ugaki's wartime diary *Fading Victory* (published posthumously).

Well-researched secondary sources include John Prados' *Combined Fleet Decoded*; Clark G. Reynolds' *The Fast Carriers*; David Hobbs' *The British Pacific Fleet*; William T. Y'Blood's *The Little Giants*; John Lambert's *The Pineapple Air Force*; and Russell Spurr's *A Glorious Way to Die*. Insightful biographies of prominent American commanders include Thomas Buell's *The Quiet Warrior* (Spruance); Theodore Taylor's *The Magnificent Mitscher*; and Admiral Halsey's autobiography *Admiral Halsey's Story*.

Among Osprey Publishing's subject-related titles are Derrick Wright's *Iwo Jima 1945*; Gordon Rottman's *Okinawa 1945*; Edward Young's *American Aces Against the Kamikazes*; Mike Yeo's *Desperate Sunset*; Mark Stille's *US Navy Carrier Aircraft vs IJN Yamato Class Battleships*; and this author's *The Naval Siege of Japan 1945*.

ACRONYMS AND ABBREVIATIONS

APD	high-speed transport (hull classification)		LCM(R)	landing craft mechanized (rocket)
ARL	landing craft repair ship		LCS(L)	landing craft support (large)
ARS	rescue and salvage ship		LCT	landing craft (tank)
ASL	above sea level		LSD	landing ship (dock)
avgas	aviation fuel		LSM(R)	landing ship medium (rocket)
CAP	Combat Air Patrol		LST	landing ship (tank)
CAS	close air support		LSV	landing ship (vehicle)
CASCU	Commander Air Support Control Units		MAG	Marine aircraft group
CIC	Combat Information Center		nm	nautical mile
CVE	escort carrier (hull classification)		OS2U	Vought OS2U Kingfisher floatplane
D-Day	Invasion of Iwo Jima		PBM	patrol bomber (Martin PBM Mariner)
DD	destroyer (hull classification)		PC	patrol craft
DE	destroyer escort (hull classification)		PCE	patrol craft escort
DM	destroyer minelayer (hull classification)		PGM	motor gunboat
DMS	destroyer minesweeper (hull classification)		RAPCAP	Radar Picket Combat Air Patrol
L-Day	Invasion of Okinawa		RPS	radar picket station
F4F	Grumman F4F Wildcat carrier-based fighter aircraft		SC	submarine chaser
			SOWESPAC	South-West Pacific Command Air Force
F4U	Vought F4U Corsair carrier-based fighter aircraft		SS	submarine (hull classification)
			TAF	(Tenth Army) Tactical Air Force
F6F	Grumman F6F Hellcat carrier-based fighter aircraft		TBF	torpedo bomber Grumman TBF Avenger
			TBM	torpedo bomber Grumman TBM Avenger
FM	fighter aircraft		TF	Task Force
FAW	fleet airwing		TG	Task Group
G4M Betty	Mitsubishi Navy Type 1 medium bomber		UDT	Underwater Demolition Team
IGHQ	Imperial General Headquarters (Japanese high command)		USAAF	United States Army Air Forces
			USMC	United States Marine Corps
IJA	Imperial Japanese Army		USN	United States Navy
IJAAF	Imperial Japanese Army Air Force		VC	escort carrier
IJN	Imperial Japanese Navy		VH	rescue squadron
IJNAF	Imperial Japanese Navy Air Force		VMF	Marine fighting squadron
JICPOA	Joint Intelligence Intelligence Center		VMF(N)	Marine night fighter squadron
Ki-61 Tony	Kawasaki Ki-61 Hien Army Type 3 fighter		VMO	Marine observation squadron
LCI(G)	landing craft infantry (guns)		VMTB	Marine torpedo bombing squadron
LCI(M)	landing craft infantry (medium)		VPB	patrol bombing squadron
LCI(R)	landing craft infantry (rocket)		YMS	auxiliary motor minesweeper

INDEX